The Christian, the Court, and the Constitution
Your Rights as a Christian Citizen
by
Jay Alan Sekulow

About the Author

Jay Alan Sekulow is Chief Counsel of the American Center for Law and Justice and the European Centre for Law and Justice and the Slavic Center for Law and Justice. Mr. Sekulow begins the new millenium by arguing two landmark First Amendment cases before the U.S. Supreme Court — bringing to nine the number of times he has appeared before the Supreme Court to defend the rights of Christians to express their faith at school, in the workplace, and in the public arena.

He received his bachelor's degree and his doctor of jurisprudence from Mercer University, where he graduated cum laude and served as an editorial staff member on the *Mercer Law Review.*

A nationally recognized and respected defender of religious freedom, Mr. Sekulow comments frequently on issues affecting people of faith and the American family and is often quoted in national news publications like *USA Today, Washington Post, New York Times,* and *ABA Journal.* He also appears regularly on national television and radio news programs including *The 700 Club.*

Twice the *National Law Journal* has named Mr. Sekulow as one of the "100 Most Influential Lawyers" in the United States. He has also been recognized by *The American Lawyer* as one of the distinguished attorneys in a group known as "The Public Sector 45."

The magazine said the designation represents "45 young lawyers outside the private sector whose vision and commitment are changing lives." He is the author of several books and hosts a daily radio program, *Jay Sekulow Live!*, which is broadcast in more than 100 markets nationwide.

About the ACLJ

The American Center for Law and Justice is a not-for-profit public interest law firm and educational organization dedicated to the promotion of pro-liberty, pro-life, and pro-family causes.

The ACLJ engages in litigation, provides legal services, renders advice and counsel to clients, and supports attorneys who are involved in defending the religious and civil liberties of Americans.

As a not-for-profit organization that does not charge for its legal services, the American Center for Law and Justice is dependent upon God and the resources He provides through the time, talent, and gifts of thousands of people who share our commitment to defend the religious and civil liberties of people of faith.

If you have a specific question about your religious freedoms, contact us:

The American Center for Law and Justice
P. O. Box 64429
Virginia Beach, Virginia 23467-4429
Phone 757-226-2489
Fax 757-226-2836
Webpage address: www.aclj.org

Acknowledgements

We would like to thank the thousands of people who support the mission of the American Center for Law and Justice. Their financial support and their prayers make our legal and our educational work possible.

TABLE OF CONTENTS

4

Introduction

As the American Center for Law and Justice begins its second decade of service, I want to assure you that the ACLJ remains committed and dedicated to defending religious freedom in America. We have been privileged to assist hundreds of thousands of people in protecting their First Amendment rights of religious speech and expression during our first ten years of operation. Now, as we embark on the next ten years, we will work even harder to make sure your religious freedoms are protected - at work, at home, at school, in the public arena.

I am delighted to present to you this book, *The Christian, the Court, and the Constitution*, which is a compilation of two publications produced by the ACLJ that have already become an important resource for thousands of Americans. By combining our popular publications, *Knowing Your Rights* and *Christian Rights in the Workplace,* we are delighted to offer you one publication that provides the critical information you need to know in defending your constitutionally protected liberties. I have also included the opening chapter from my book, *From Intimidation to Victory,* that details my own spiritual journey and commitment to serving the Lord.

As the Chief Counsel of the American Center for Law and Justice, I have received hundreds of thousands of requests for assistance from people who believe their rights have been violated. Many of these requests relate to religious expression in the public schools, religious discrimination in the workplace, and the right to share views publicly — whether that means sharing the Gospel or addressing contemporary issues from a biblical viewpoint.

In the pages that follow, I provide answers to many of the recurring questions that we receive daily at the American Center for Law and Justice. My answers are based on general legal principles that may or may not apply to any given situation. Because each actual case is unique, the specific facts of each case have a direct impact on its outcome. So the answers here will give you general guidance, but you need to seek professional legal counsel to address the specifics of your situation.

My heartfelt desire is that this book will help you understand your rights — in language that is easy to read and easy to understand.

As we begin this new millenium, we must continue to work for true liberty in America. We are committed to that mission at the ACLJ.

Jay Alan Sekulow
January 2000

Section One

FROM INTIMIDATION TO VICTORY

It is amazing how the Lord makes Himself present to you in your life. I want to share with you the opening chapter from my 1990 book, *From Intimidation to Victory*, a chapter that chronicles my first argument before the U.S. Supreme Court and my spiritual journey that led me to understand and accept Jesus as my Messiah.

I think I know why they call it the "high court." Start climbing those steps outside the United States Supreme Court and you feel as if you're hiking up to heaven. Pretty intimidating for a first-time visitor (and one with short legs, at that).

I ascended those steps for the first time in 1987. The brief time it took to move from the sidewalk to the inner sanctum of the nation's highest court paralleled the rapid unfolding of what was to become a cutting-edge ministry. It's a calling that would more than once bring me back to Washington, D.C., to defend religious freedom before the Supreme Court.

As I walked up the steps, I thought how God must have a sense of humor. A few years ago nobody - including me - would have suspected a Brooklyn-born Jew, then only thirty-one years old and a Christian, would be arguing before the Supreme Court for the right of Christians to evangelize in public airports.

I arrived early and adjusted the podium for my five-foot, seven-inch frame. The last thing I needed was any handicaps, such as having to stand tiptoe to address the court. I knew that after six months of consuming preparation the skirmish would be intense but brief. Thirty minutes of back and forth with the justices, and winner take all.

Hanging in the balance was the opportunity to witness in the midst of millions of people. *Literally hundreds of millions.* The case had originated with the threatened arrest of a Jews for Jesus missionary at Los Angeles International Airport, where thirty-five million people pass through in one year. In Atlanta, Georgia, where I live, the airport handles forty-two million a year. Many of these people are lonely, sitting around with time to spare, very open to the gospel. I knew the Bill of Rights, specifically the First Amendment, guaranteed the freedom to talk about Jesus with them. Who knows how many salvations, how many eternal destinies, would be affected by the decision of these nine justices?

Recognizing the Suffering Servant

So how did a Jewish kid from Brooklyn get involved with justices and Jesus? It certainly wasn't something I planned.

I was born in 1956 in Brooklyn but eventually moved to Long Island and lived there until my teen years. My family attended a Reform synagogue. I liked Friday night Sabbath services, though we attended only about once a month. Hebrew school was a different story. I think the only reason the cantor didn't expel my friend and me for misbehavior was that my friend's dad had donated the synagogue's plush drapes.

Religion was not a big topic of discussion in our home. Sometimes my father referred to the Supreme Being, but usually only at the holidays. I remember, when I was thirteen, trading insults over religion with a Catholic friend. We never got too serious about it, but I remember wondering if he was right. Could Jesus be the Messiah?

The thought left as quickly as it had come. I was secure in my Jewish identity, which excluded Jesus as redeemer. Though my family wasn't too religious, we reinforced our heritage by celebrating the Jewish holidays. My *bar mitzvah*, at age thirteen, was a glorious day: the end of Hebrew school and my passage into adulthood.

Two years later my family moved to Atlanta. My high school grades there ranked with my reading of the Torah at *bar mitzvah* - mediocre. It wasn't so much dullness or laziness on my part; it was just a lack of motivation. As for hard work, I liked it. I was night manager for a large department store by the time I was seventeen. But as far as working on *grades*, well, that had to wait until college.

I planned to attend a two-year school for some business education courses, then go back to work. But a short stint at the local junior college whetted my appetite for learning. I decided to enroll in a four-year school. Little did I know the full spectrum of what I was to learn.

My desire to stay in Atlanta was probably the main reason I looked into Atlanta Baptist College (later known as Mercer University). The friendly, small-campus atmosphere was appealing. And it was only a five-minute drive from our home.

I asked my dad, "Will it bother you if I go to a school that calls itself a Baptist College?"

"Baptist-schmaptist," he said. "I'm glad you decided on a four-year college. Go ahead - get yourself a good education."

So I enrolled, determined to outsmart all the Christians. I did well in my pre-law studies. I attacked the mandatory Bible classes with a cynical confidence. I knew I could disprove the notion that Jesus was the Messiah.

What I hadn't counted on was Glenn Borders. Glenn wore a giant cross around his neck. I immediately labeled him a "Jesus freak." When we talked, though, I forgot about the big wooden cross - maybe because Glenn wasn't trying to shove it down my throat. He was active in college sports and student government and was a good student. He was there to help if you needed him. It was partly due to our friendship that my competitive attitude toward Bible courses changed to an attitude of genuine curiosity.

Glenn suggested I read Isaiah 53. The chapter scrambled my mind with its description of the "suffering servant" who sounded so much like Jesus. I must be misreading the text, I thought. Then it hit me - I had been reading from the King James Bible, a "Christian" translation. No wonder it fit so neatly. So I checked the Jewish text, but the description seemed just as clear. Still there had to be a logical explanation. No need to worry.

After I researched the rabbinic interpretations, I began to worry. Some of the earlier writings described the text as a messianic prophecy. OK, but who's the Messiah? Other Jewish scholars identified Isaiah or the nation of Israel as the suffering servant, but these contrivances were embarrassing. The details obviously described someone other than Isaiah or Israel.

I kept looking for another explanation, but nothing turned up. In the meantime, my Christian friends were suggesting that I read other passages, such as Daniel 9, which prophesies the Messiah's arrival. I went so far as to read the New Testament, which Jews are told is an extremely anti-Semitic "forbidden book." It didn't strike me as anti-Semitic. The Apostles were saying the same thing about my people that Isaiah and everybody else had said: that we were stubborn and not very obedient.

As I kept reading, my suspicion was confirmed that

Jesus really was the Messiah. But the decision was purely intellectual. I had wrestled with the question for about a year and was glad finally to put the matter to rest. I realized I needed a Messiah who would die as a sin-bearer, and I was grateful to have one. But for me to respond? That didn't occur to me.

A few days later I heard the Jews for Jesus singing group, The Liberated Wailing Wall. What a relief it was to see other Jews who believed that Jesus was the Messiah! Their music and message helped me realize that if I really believed in Jesus I needed to make a commitment to Him. They gave an altar call. I responded. It was February 1975. I was eighteen.

That night a lady I'd never met said, "If you get kicked out of your home tonight, you can stay with us." She caught me off guard. I had always had a good relationship with my parents - didn't smoke, drink or use dope. It hadn't entered my mind that my parents might be upset. After all, Jesus was a Jew. I was a Jew. What's the big deal if I wanted to believe Jesus was the Jewish Messiah?

The woman's remark scared me, and I decided not to tell my parents anything at first. But I woke up at 2:00 A.M., unable to sleep. I was close to my parents; I couldn't withhold such a major decision from them.

So I woke my father. I told him I had decided Jesus was our Messiah.

"You decided?" he said groggily. Of course, he was implying, Who are you to decide? He shook his head and said, "We'll talk about it in the morning."

Morning came, and he said nothing about it. Neither did I. Since I was living under their roof, I felt if they didn't want to discuss it, I should leave well enough alone. I had already been receiving Jews for

Jesus literature at the house, so they knew this was more than a passing incident. We eventually discussed Jesus, yet they have never been hostile about my beliefs. They know I'm still Jewish. They know no cult has wrapped its tentacles around my brain and caused drastic personality changes.

Law School's Back Door

I finished undergraduate school with tremendous grades, but my law school admission test grade was low. Every time I took a review course I would score ten points less, so I decided not to take it anymore.

My first law school interview was with Mercer's law school dean. He said, " I don't care what they tell you after you go to the faculty interview - you be here the first day school starts.

The faculty interview ripped me to shreds. "You'll never make it here," they said.

The faculty encounter left me crushed, so the first day of law school found me at work at the department store. At 6:00 A.M. the law school dean called and screamed at me for fifteen minutes.

"I get one student a year just for whatever reason I want, and you were the one I picked. I told you to be here. Now get down here!" This time I took the hint. I went on to graduate second in my class.

I say all this not to boast but to show that God was preparing me for something. I had no idea what. But He doesn't give us five-year plans all the time. He often unfolds things bit by bit. If He chooses to jerk me out of a department store job and drop me in law school, that's His way. I can't argue. And God can surprise any one of us like that if we're completely open to serve Him.

I began my career in law as a tax prosecutor for the Internal Revenue Service. In one sense it was a miserable job; prosecuting people for fraud and tax evasion does not win you any popularity contests. But the trial experience can launch you into a terrific career if you win your cases - and I did.

I left the IRS to begin a law practice with a friend from law school. We had a monthly overhead of $1,600 and not one client. But with God's help we soon found business. We won some controversial cases and developed a good reputation. In less than eight months my firm was up to nine lawyers, two full-time certified public accountants and three paralegals.

While the law firm grew, I branched into a construction business. It occupied five floors of a downtown office building and was extremely successful.

Putting Up a Fight

As business flourished, so did my family. I had married Pam after my first year in law school, on my birthday, June 10, 1978. We had two sons, Jordan and Logan.

Meanwhile, I stayed in touch with Jews for Jesus. Though I began serving on their board of directors, I still was not giving vent to a desire that was growing in me: to use my legal skills to serve God.

Jews for Jesus had been distributing gospel tracts at the Los Angeles International Airport for fourteen years. For no apparent reason, one day police threatened the arrest of one of their missionaries. I was asked to represent them.

"Look, get a lawyer in Los Angeles," I said. "The

case won't go too far, and every court in the United States has decided that airports are appropriate for evangelism. My goodness, they let in the Moonies and every other group that solicits money and does everything else. So why are they picking on an evangelist?"

I would come to know why two years later in Washington, D.C.

In the interim, people kept telling me they sensed that God wanted me involved in this case. No way, I said. Then suddenly our large construction business dried up -- tax-code changes hit, and in three months it evaporated, with all three hundred employees out of work. We had lost everything, even our home. While we were financially bankrupt, God chose this time to reach down to me, it took getting to the point where I could no longer control things.

I finally got the message. I spent the next six months preparing for a thirty-minute rendezvous with the Supreme Court.

When I was in Washington, I asked the Los Angeles city attorney why this case had gone all the way to the Supreme Court. He told me the reason - and this is an indictment of me and all American Christians - was that the airport commissioners *did not think Christians would put up a fight.* They had a regulation to test, so why not pick on the pious, placid Christians, who would do nothing more than fold their hands and fret?

Before the Supreme Court proceedings began, I looked back at the "Christian row." There were my wife, Jews for Jesus representatives - and my parents. Whatever their feelings were about my beliefs, they were there to support me. And most important, God's presence was there. My wife, Pam, agreed that there

15

was a supernatural peace and confidence in my presentation.

The city attorney went first. The justices sliced him alive with their questioning. It got so bad that — no kidding — I even prayed for the guy. It began to look good for us, yet I knew to expect no tea party when my turn came.

I was all set to launch into an eloquent Americana speech, our heritage of free speech and all that, but the questions started. The justices didn't stop firing for thirty minutes.

The court unanimously upheld the decisions of the lower courts that the airport's resolution to curtail First Amendment rights was unconstitutional. The passive Christians had fought back and won.

One of the big legal periodicals, *American Lawyer*, reviewed the case and judged my presentation "rude, aggressive and obnoxious." I decided this was accurate, or almost so. I don't think I was obnoxious — maybe rude, since I cut the chief justice off while he was speaking, but that was OK. Since he didn't give me a chance to do my opening, and there were only two minutes left, I was certainly going to deliver my closing.

Rude and aggressive? Yes. If you really believe what the Bible says — that Jesus is the only way, that outside our comfortable church buildings there is a world full of drifting souls, doomed to hell -- then you have to be aggressive. Sometimes you have to be rude.

Actually, so often it's not the *messenger* who's rude and obnoxious, it's the *message*. Or, more precisely, it's the reception of the message. Those needing to hear the gospel are in the grip of Satan. If you enjoy darkness, even a little light is going to annoy you. Because so many people find the gospel annoying, those in powerful positions have no qualms about making evangelism illegal because it strikes them as rude and obnoxious. Consequently, it's become increasingly difficult for Christians to share that message with the freedom they have traditionally had.

To help Christians share the message of hope and love found in Jesus Christ, I began a lifelong commitment to defend the rights of Christians protected by the U.S. Constitution.

Before joining the American Center for Law and Justice, I launched a legal advocacy group called Christian Advocates Serving Evangelism (CASE) which has since become the Atlanta chapter (or office) of the ACLJ.

My commitment to safeguarding the rights of people of faith is stronger today than it has ever been. While we have seen great success at all levels of the judiciary - including the U.S. Supreme Court - it is clear there is still much work to be done in ensuring that the First Amendment rights of Christians are protected at home, at school, in the workplace, and in the public arena.

Section Two

PUBLIC PLACES: Christians in the Marketplace of Ideas

Chapter One

Taking the Gospel to the Streets

Taking the Gospel to the streets is a commission and a commandment for believers. Responding obediently to the Commission and hitting the streets, we receive grace and power to fulfill the Lord's commands. Hitting the streets always has had a personal cost. Consider the price paid by Stephen, who became the first martyr for preaching the Gospel. And remember Peter, James and John, who preached in the name of Jesus, even though threatened with imprisonment.

Today, however, American Christians face no such cost for preaching the Gospel. The streets and sidewalks of the United States are an open forum for evangelism.

Isn't it strange that when the time comes to hit the streets, many Christians with willing hearts hesitate for fear that their preaching may result in arrest and prosecution. True, from time to time those who preach the Gospel are challenged by government officials regarding the use of public streets, parks and sidewalks for evangelism activities. But, as a general rule, such fears are unfounded.

In the following pages, we show how the Constitution guarantees your right to preach the Gospel in public places. For over 60 years, the Supreme Court has examined cases involving preaching (or other speech activities) on the streets. These cases provide ready answers to those who challenge your right to take the Gospel to the streets.

Q What do you mean by "taking the Gospel to the streets?"

A Taking the Gospel to the streets means using written and unspoken words to tell the man or woman on the street about Jesus. Taking the Gospel to the streets means giving away tracts, pamphlets, and other printed material that presents the Gospel. Taking the Gospel to the streets means speaking to people on the streets — telling them about the Lord and his free gift of salvation.

Q What laws protect my right to take the Gospel to the streets?

A When you give away Gospel tracts in public places — streets, sidewalks and parks — you are engaged in a form of speech and publication protected by the United States Constitution and civil rights laws. When you speak with someone about the Gospel while in a public place, you enjoy constitutional protection.

The laws of this nation and of your state, which protect other forms of speech and press, protect your rights to evangelize. As American citizens, we are protected by the United States Constitution from government interference with our right of free speech. Also, the Constitutions of every state in our country include guarantees of free speech, which are at least as protective of free speech as the American Constitution. Some state constitutions (including California and New Jersey) are more protective of speech than the First Amendment.

The First Amendment to the United States Constitution says:

"Congress shall make no law . . . abridging the freedom of speech . . . ." The Fourteenth Amendment says: "nor shall any State deprive any person of life, liberty, or property, without due process of law . . . ."

The Supreme Court has ruled that these two parts of the Constitution severely limit the power of federal, state, and local governments to interfere with speech activities on sidewalks, streets, and in parks.

Q When I have handed out Gospel literature in the past, police have stopped me and told me that soliciting is not allowed. Am I soliciting when I share the Gospel?

A No! Giving away free Gospel tracts and talking to people about salvation are not the same thing as soliciting. The Supreme Court recently decided a case involving the difference between soliciting and leafletting. In the *Kokinda* case, the Supreme Court permitted the postal service to enforce a rule against asking (soliciting) for donations on postal property. In that case, political activists were asking for donations while standing on a sidewalk leading from the post office building to the post office parking lot.

However, the court suggested that it would reject a rule that banned free distribution of literature on such properties. Discussing the difference, the Court said,

As residents of metropolitan areas know from daily experience, confrontation by a person asking for money disrupts passage and is more intrusive and

intimidating than an encounter with a person giving out information. One need not ponder the contents of a leaflet or pamphlet in order mechanically to take it out of someone's hand, but one must listen, comprehend, decide and act in order to respond to a solicitation. [1]

In the *ISKCON, Inc. v. Lee* and *Lee v. ISKCON, Inc* cases, the Supreme Court considered a restriction on leafletting and another restriction on solicitation of donations in airport terminals operated by the Port Authority of New York and New Jersey. The Court concluded that, despite the fact that the airport terminals were nonpublic forums, a regulation barring the distribution of free literature in the terminals was unreasonable and unconstitutional. The Court also held that solicitation is separate from literature distribution and can thereby be banned, even though literature distribution cannot be banned.

ISKCON together with *Kokinda* reinforce the concept that solicitation and the distribution of literature are separate. While a city official may, in some instances, not allow solicitation, such a regulation may not be broadened to include literature distribution.

As long as you are giving away your literature for free, and you aren't panhandling for donations, you are engaging in the most protected form of speech. That does not mean that you will never have problems. Although it is often just an excuse for stopping street evangelism, this is one of

21

the objections to leafletting we hear about most frequently. It often takes a strongly worded letter to attorneys for the city or county involved to resolve the problem.

Q Where can I go to hand out Gospel tracts to the public?

A You can go to any publicly owned street, sidewalk or park. In legal terms, streets, sidewalks and parks are "traditional public forums." That means that these are the places people traditionally relate to public speeches or leafletting; we are accustomed to the presence of newspaper boxes and paperboys on public sidewalks; we expect the candidates in an upcoming election to hold their rallies at the park; and we assume that when some group is unhappy about something they are likely to march down a nearby street.

None of these activities surprise us. Why? Because streets, sidewalks and parks are traditionally connected to our history and experience of free speech activities.

Sometimes a city official will get confused about these "traditional public forums." For example, in *Frisby v. Schultz* (487 U.S. 474) the Supreme Court rejected a Wisconsin city's argument that the streets and sidewalks of a residential area were not the sort of "traditional public forums" that the Court had held were generally open to free speech and activities. In that case, the Court showed that it was no longer acceptable for governments to make such arguments because, in the Court's view, a street is a street is a street. The Court noted that the kinds of regulations that would be permissible varied with the nature of the streets at issue. For example, a rule against parades between sunset and sunrise on residential streets serves a valid purpose of protecting the peace of a neighborhood during a time when most residents are resting. A rule against a noisy activity on a hospital street or on a street near a school during school hours are other examples of reasonable rules.

You are not limited to streets, parks and sidewalks for tract distribution. Courts have found many other places to be appropriate. Airport terminals and bus and train stations have all been found by courts to be appropriate locations for leafletting. The walkways and sidewalks surrounding government-owned coliseums and stadiums are also appropriate. Many tourist attractions around the country are appropriate locations, as well. For example, the walkways and paths surrounding the Washington Monument and the Vietnam Veterans Memorial are protected.

Q When witnessing, sometimes I am on a sidewalk in front of a business. I have had police officers tell me that I must move away from a business or that I must keep moving or I will be "loitering." Is this right?

A No! "Loitering" means that you have no legitimate purpose or business for being in a certain place. But your evangelism activities are a legitimate purpose for standing on a sidewalk. Of course, if you try standing in the middle of the street, you may run into a different problem. (But that problem is obstructing the flow of traffic, not "loitering.") The loitering charge, when made against a street evangelist who is actively preaching the Gospel, is invalid.

Of course, you don't have the right to barricade a sidewalk, allowing only those who will take a tract to pass. Your right to use the sidewalks, streets and parks is not a license to make them unusable for others. Besides, how effective will your preaching be if you anger those around you by treating them rudely or blocking their way?

Q I don't live in the town where I want to hand out Gospel tracts and preach on the streets. Police tell me that I don't have the same rights when visiting a town or state away from home. Is this right?

A You are not limited to the streets, sidewalks and parks in your town. Many cases which we have brought involve visitors from other towns or other states. The constitutional rule is that state and local governments cannot treat visitors from out of town or another state differently than local residents.

Q I want to get started witnessing to the Good News of the Gospel. What should I do?

A First, devote time to prayer and prayerful preparation.

Next, select a target. You may choose some particular place because of the opportunity to reach many people — outside a sports stadium or near an historic monument. You may have a target group in mind. For example, if your burden is for young people, you will want to select locations where young people pass by or gather.

If the location you

choose is not a nice, simple sidewalk location, you should speak to the appropriate authority to discover what rules have been adopted to govern your activities. (This does not mean that you must always accept, like the Ten Commandments, a rule barring leafletting.) Check with a county clerk, the police department, the security office at the stadium or similar offices. This will let you know what to expect when you witness. Of course, if you are in a public place and are stopped from distributing free Gospel literature, do not assume that it was correct for you to be stopped. Too many Supreme Court cases have been decided against governments on these matters to assume that government is always right. Many seemingly hopeless cases in which leafletters ultimately fight will cause many government units to change policies.

Chapter Two
Lamb's Chapel and the Use of Public Facilities

The victory obtained in the *Lamb's Chapel* case marked an important turning point for Christians obtaining access to the marketplace of ideas. In a unanimous decision, the Court held that religious organizations confronting contemporary issues from a religious perspective cannot be excluded from access to government property available to other groups. No longer can Christians be treated as second-class citizens. [2]

Q What is the *Lamb's Chapel* case?
A The facts in the *Lamb's Chapel* case were straightforward. An

evangelical church desired to rent a school facility for an evening showing of a film series produced by Dr. James Dobson's Focus on the Family ministry. The film series, entitled "Turn Your Heart Toward Home," dealt with contemporary family issues from a biblical perspective. The church's request for use was denied by school administrators because it was "church related." Although the school facilities were available to community groups for social, civic, and recreational purposes, the rules and regulations specifically prohibited any religious use. The Supreme Court ruled against this prohibition, stating that the religious exclusion was unconstitutional.

Q What is the impact of the *Lamb's Chapel* case?

A In many cities and counties throughout the United States, local school facilities are the town halls of the community. Access to these town halls is essential for Christians who want to have issues addressed from their perspective. Although many in a community may not feel comfortable going to a church to hear a presentation on a contemporary issue, people do feel at ease attending meetings held in community facilities such as school auditoriums and civic centers. The impact of the *Lamb's Chapel* case is significant. Every government agency, from school boards to city councils, that has access policies in place for its properties must now allow Christians to utilize those facilities as well. We must take advantage of this new openness in the marketplace the *Lamb's Chapel* case has created.

Q Does *Lamb's Chapel* only apply to churches?

A No. Although the particular case before the Supreme Court involved the Lamb's Chapel church, now other community groups that want to address issues from a Christian perspective also have access to government facilities that are open to the public for use. For instance, in Mobile, Alabama, an evangelistic ministry known as "Strike Force International" is now entitled to have an evangelistic crusade at the public school in Alabama because of an access policy that had to be modified in light of *Lamb's Chapel*. Evangelistic events can now take place in school facilities in the evening as well as in city halls or other government facilities open to general use.

Q Does *Lamb's Chapel* only apply to school facilities?

A No. The decision in *Lamb's Chapel* applies to *any* government facility, whether a town hall, civic center, or city hall, that is open to the general public for social, civic, or recreational uses. We have found that most cities across America have access policies to local government buildings for community use. We have also found that most of these cities specifically prohibit religious groups from utilizing these facilities. This religious exclusion is unconstitutional in light of the *Lamb's Chapel* decision.

Q What topics can be discussed when using government facilities?

A In *Lamb's Chapel*, the Supreme Court specifically noted that the purpose of the James Dobson film series was to address contemporary family issues from a Christian perspective. But the decision goes much further. Family issues, baccalaureate services for students, evangelistic events, and discussion of contemporary Christian issues can now take place in government facilities because of the decision in *Lamb's Chapel*. No longer can the excuse of church/state separation be utilized to prohibit Christians from obtaining access to this new marketplace for the presentation of ideas.

Q What about policies that still prohibit use of government facilities by Christians?
A It is time for Christians to go on the offensive and have our voices heard. This will require utilizing the rights that we just obtained from the

Supreme Court decision. Unfortunately, many cities are slow to change, and there are still hundreds of policies on the books throughout the United States which specifically prohibit religious groups from utilizing government facilities that are open to the community at large. At The American Center for Law and Justice, we have undertaken a project to have these laws removed and modified so they conform with *Lamb's Chapel*.

The procedure to gain access to a public facility is straightforward. First, if you decide you are going to utilize facilities, you must fill out an application form that is available at the seat of the local city government. Be forthright in the application, and state specifically what purpose you are going to utilize the facilities for. If the policy still prohibits religious uses, ask the city administrators if they are familiar with the *Lamb's Chapel* case. If they are not, we would be happy to send a letter on your behalf to clarify for the city government what the decision in the Supreme Court means. If you continue to have problems gaining access, we have sent demand letters — letters which state the law and inform the city officials what they must do to comply with the law — to city officials in order to obtain access. Generally, the demand letter resolves the situation. However, if we find that the demand letter is being ignored and your rights are still being denied, we can then proceed immediately to federal court and obtain an injunction, which will require the city officials to allow you to utilize the facilities under their control.

We have already seen the fruit from the decision in *Lamb's Chapel*. As I said, in Alabama the *Lamb's Chapel* decision made it possible for an evangelistic event for teenagers to proceed in a local school facility. In Wisconsin, an organization that wanted to present a six-part series on the Christian heritage of our nation was also allowed to meet after the *Lamb's Chapel* decisions came down. By utilizing government facilities and inviting the public to attend meetings where our view is presented, we gain access to an important arena and marketplace where ideas compete for minds and hearts. This is where we need to be, carrying Christianity into the fray where it can go head-to-head with other world views and demonstrate its intellectual and practical superiority.

Chapter Three
Picqueting and Demonstrating

The following questions address the right to demonstrate in the specific context of the abortion industry. Other citizen-activist groups can apply the principles discussed (for example, as they consider expressing their opposition to the sales and distribution of pornographic materials). A prominent example of such citizen outcry outside the abortion context was the national wave of public protests against the theatrical release of the movie "The Last Temptation of Christ."

The city where we live has an abortion business in it. Our local right-to-life group has developed a public information campaign to make our community aware of the nature of that business. As part of our campaign, we will be going to the public streets and sidewalks near the abortion business to express our opposition to abortion and to share lifegiving alternatives to abortion with the business patrons. We have a few questions about this plan:

Q May we express our opposition to abortion and offer alternatives to it by going personally to the public areas around the business's locale?

A Yes. You may express your views about abortion while in the vicinity of abortion businesses. There are some important points to bear in mind when engaged in such activities.

Remember that there is a legal difference between the streets, sidewalks and parks of a community, and the private property owned by another citizen. A key difference is that streets, sidewalks and parks, including those located near abortion businesses, have historically been a place where citizens gather to discuss and debate issues of public importance. The Supreme Court has said that streets, sidewalks and parks "have immemorially been held in trust for the use of the public and, time out of mind, have been used for purposes of assembly, communicating thoughts between citizens, and discussing public questions." [3] So, to stay within the bounds of the law, your activities must occur on the publicly owned streets, sidewalks and parks.

Bear in mind that your city council or county commission can regulate, in certain narrow and specific ways, the time, place, and manner of such activities. For example, a city may enforce a rule against obstructing passage on a public sidewalk or against excessive noise. The Supreme Court has said that the right to engage in expressive activities in public places is not an absolute right and that it "must be exercised in . . . peace and good order." [4] Because rights to freedom of speech, press, and assembly are supremely precious, even such laws as those barring obstructions or excessive noise are closely reviewed by courts to ensure that "in the guise of regulation" the government does not seek to "abridge or deny" such rights. [5]

Q We are planning a march around the city block where the abortion business is located. We expect more than 100 participants. When we spoke to the city manager's office, we were told that we had to apply for a permit to engage in this activity. Do we have to obtain a permit?

A Perhaps. As noted above, cities can impose reasonable regulations of time, place and manner on speech activities. The Supreme Court has held that the requirement of a permit for a parade or march can be just such a reasonable regulation of speech. At the same time, the Supreme Court has held that governments which impose a requirement of prior permission have imposed a "prior restraint" on speech. Cities that impose such "prior restraints" bear a heavy burden to justify their use. For example, in one recent case, the Supreme Court struck down a parade permit rule because the rule allowed the city to impose greater costs on marches by persons expressing unpopular views. [6]

You should check with the police department or the city manager's office for information on, and a copy of, any ordinance affecting the right to conduct a demonstration or march. If the requirements set out in such ordinances seem burdensome or inappropriate, seek out legal counsel on whether the ordinance is constitutional.

Q We also plan to distribute written materials on

abortion. We have been told that we are not allowed to solicit in this manner and that we cannot distribute leaflets because of the litter that results. Do we have the right to distribute literature while we are on the public streets and sidewalks?

A Yes. You have the right, in almost every circumstance conceivable, to distribute written materials which express your views on any issue, including abortion. Some misguided bureaucrats may presume that, by calling the distribution of pamphlets "solicitation," they will be able to undermine your right to leaflet. But the Supreme Court has treated leafletting as an activity distinct from solicitation. Leafletting is a well-established model of protected expression. It is a constitutional axiom that distributing written materials in public is a protected exercise of the rights of freedom of speech and press.[7] The Supreme court has said that, unlike other activities such as oral solicitations for money or business, the distribution is an unobtrusive form of communication.[8]

If you have experienced evangelistic or political literature distribution, then you know, as do thousands of "residents of metropolitan areas, [that] confrontation by a person asking for money disrupts passage and is more intrusive and intimidating than an encounter with a person giving out information."[9] Leafletting is unobtrusive because the recipient "need not ponder the contents of a leaflet or pamphlet in order mechanically to take it out of someone's hand . . . ."[10]

Nor may your city justifiably treat leafletting as a crime. Long ago, the Supreme Court declared unconstitutional a city ordinance which prohibited leafletting in order to prevent the problems associated with litter. [11] A city's desire to keep the streets clean and the sewers unclogged, the Supreme Court has said, "is insufficient to justify an ordinance which prohibits a person rightfully on a public street from handing literature to one willing to receive it." [12] Rather than silencing those who are exercising the constitutional rights to freedom of speech and of the press, your city must address its fears about litter by punishing those who litter, not those who leaflet.

Chapter Four

Organizing National Days of Prayer Rallies

On the National Day of Prayer, I would like to coordinate a public prayer service on the plaza in front of the county court-house and government center. I know this area has been used for arts festivals, craft fairs, and political campaign events, among other things. When I requested to use the plaza for an hour-long prayer service, my request was denied. I was told that "separa-tion of church and state" would be violated if prayer were permitted on the county-owned plaza. I have some questions:

Q Will I violate the Establishment

Clause of the Constitution if I sponsor a prayer service on the National Day of Prayer on the courthouse plaza?

A No. Unless you *are* the government or its representative, you cannot violate the Establishment Clause. On its face, the Establishment Clause only restricts the United States Congress from making laws "respecting an Establishment of Religion." The Supreme Court has interpreted another part of the Constitution, the Fourteenth Amendment, to impose the same limitations on state governments which the Establishment Clause imposes on Congress. But the Supreme Court has never held, nor could it sensibly hold, that private persons can violate the Establishment Clause.

Moreover, when your county government bars you from using a public place, such as the courthouse plaza, because of the religious nature of your planned activity, your county is violating the Establishment Clause by showing hostility toward religion. If the plaza is open for public use and access, and if the plaza has been used for such things as art festivals, craft fairs, and political campaign events, then the county is barred from discriminating against your event because of religion.

Q In other communities, there isn't an open public space appropriate for the prayer service. Some of these towns have meeting rooms in public libraries or in government office buildings. Can we

have access to such public meeting rooms?

A Yes. In June 1993, the Supreme Court held that a New York school district violated the right to freedom of speech of a church and a pastor when it refused their request to use a school auditorium to publicly show a film series on contemporary family issues. [13] The school district directly stated that it was the religious nature of the planned activity that led to the denial of permission. The school district argued that its denial of a religious use of the public facilities under its control was necessary to avoid a violation of the Establishment Clause. The Supreme Court held that the school district had engaged in prohibited viewpoint discrimination. Based on the Supreme Court's holding, and assuming in your case that such public meeting rooms are open to citizen use for the purpose of discussing public issues of importance, there is no justifiable basis for excluding an event because of its religious nature.

Chapter Five
Rights Regarding Public Nativity Scenes

So many of the activities during the Christmas season have become completely secularized. Our church would like to help "Keep Christ in Christmas" by erecting a nativity scene in a popular park here in town. Here are some questions we have about this.

Q Didn't the Supreme Court rule

a few years ago that such nativity displays are unconstitutional?

A No. The Supreme Court has never said that private citizens can be barred from setting up a nativity display, or any other display of a religious nature, in a public park. In the only two cases decided by the Supreme Court, the nativity displays were either owned or maintained and promoted by the government. [14] In one case, the nativity display, which was part of a larger display with a generally secular theme, was held not to violate the Establishment Clause. [15] In the other case, the nativity display, which stood alone, was held to be a violation of the Establishment Clause. [16]

Q Can the parks department compel us to include such things as snowmen, fairies, Santa Clauses, etc., in order to emphasize secular aspects of the holiday? Can they bar us from including such wholly religious aspects as a sign saying "Keep Christ in Christmas?" Can they prohibit us from singing traditional religious Christmas music? Can they compel us to sing secular songs?

A No. No. No. No. In order to understand the legal issues involved, think of your nativity display as a message to the public. By setting up the creche, you are telling your fellow citizens to "Keep Christ in Christmas." By singing traditional, religious carols, you are showing the public how to

37

"Keep Christ in Christmas."

Viewed in this way, it becomes clear that it is inappropriate and unconstitutional for a government entity to meddle with your message. Fifty years ago, the United States Supreme Court held that a religious adherent could not be compelled to participate in a flag salute if such participation would violate rights of conscience. [17] Compelling a flag salute in such circumstances would be a presumption that a government official could prescribe orthodoxy of opinion. But, as the Supreme Court interpreted the Constitution, such a presumption was unconstitutional. The Supreme Court said, "[i]f there is any fixed star in our constitutional constellation, it is that no official high or petty, can prescribe what shall be orthodox in politics, nationalism, religion, or other matters of opinion or force citizens to confess by word or act their faith therein." [18] In like manner, a parks authority official cannot determine for you what kind of expression is appropriate in your private display.

Q Are there any new developments in the law concerning public displays of nativity scenes?

A Yes, it is constitutional when churches, community groups, civic organizations, or private individuals privately display nativity scenes, or other religious symbols, on property which is considered to be open for the use of the public, such as public squares where other displays are permitted.

The Supreme Court recently decided a case that helps clarify the law regarding nativity scenes and other public property displays of religious symbols. [19] The Court relied heavily on its decisions in *Lamb's Chapel* and *Mergens* when it held that the Ku Klux Klan had a right to display a cross on public property where other religious and secular symbols were being displayed.

Bolstering the protection of religious speech, the Court stated that "[o]ur precedent establishes that private religious speech, far from being a First Amendment orphan, is as fully protected under the Free Speech Clause as secular private expression." [20] The need to reinforce the existing Constitutional protection against hostility, that is often aimed at religious speech, was expressed by the Court when it stated that "[i]ndeed, in Anglo-American history . . . government suppression of speech has so commonly been directed precisely at religious speech that a free-speech clause without religion would be Hamlet without the prince." [21] The Court's logic was heavily influenced by the fact that the government was not endorsing the displays because the area was open to all religious and secular symbols representing private expression. [22]

Perhaps the most telling comment from the Court discusses the fact that a contrary view "exiles private religious speech to a realm of less-protected expression heretofore inhabited only by sexually explicit displays and commercial speech. It will be a sad day when this Court casts piety in with pornography, and finds the First Amendment more hospitable to private expletives, than to private prayers. This would be merely bizarre were religious speech simply as protected by the Constitution as other forms of private speech; but it is outright perverse when one considers that private religious expression receives preferential treatment under the Free Exercise Clause. It is no answer to say that the Establishment Clause tempers religious speech. By its terms that Clause applies only to the words and acts of government. It was never meant, and has never been read by this court, to serve as an impediment to purely private religious speech connected to the State only through its occurrence in a public forum." [23]   Thus, it is unlawful for religious speech or displays to be excluded from public property solely on the basis of the religious nature of that speech or display.

The Plurality concluded with a quick summary stating that "[r]eligious expression cannot violate the Establishment Clause, where it (1) is purely private and (2) occurs in a traditional or designated public forum, publicly announced and open to all on equal terms." [24]   Therefore, it is constitutional when churches, community groups, civic organizations, or private individuals privately display nativity scenes or other religious symbols on property which is considered to be open for the use of the public, such as public squares where other displays are permitted.

Chapter Six

Removing Pornography From Your Community

Communities have the right to regulate pornography according to local standards. That means they can restrict what is sold, where it is sold, and who is able to buy it. They can even prohibit pornography altogether.

Finding out who is carrying pornography is an important step toward eradicating it. Targeting convenience stores selling adult magazines, video stores renting adult movies, gift stores selling pornographic novelty items, and any other merchant that is selling sexually explicit material can be an effective way of eliminating pornography from a community. What I mean by targeting is the exercise of our First Amendment freedom of speech and freedom of assembly rights so our voices are heard.

Distributing literature, peaceful protests and picketing in objection to the materials sold in the stores are proven techniques for removing pornography. Another way of removing pornography is to stand with a camera in front of stores selling explicit pornographic materials. Many people who frequent these stores do not want their presence documented. You must understand that these particular methods could lead to explosive situations, so never protest or picket alone.

Many groups have organized boycotts through their local churches aimed at merchants selling pornographic materials. Some community activists have gone directly to the city attorney and expressed concern about pornography in the community. City attorneys have several options. First, many cities have ordinances restricting pornography and have simply failed to enforce them. By confronting city attorneys you may find that tough ordinances are already on the books and can be enforced to prohibit unlawful activity. Second, if your community lacks ordinances concerning pornography, talk with city council members about drafting appropriate laws. Other cities have done this and have been very successful in regulating and eliminating pornography. Finally, stores that sell pornographic materials can be zoned into certain areas so the materials are inaccessible to children.

National boycotts have also been effective against convenience store chains that stock soft-core pornographic magazines and against companies that advertise objectionable magazines. Do not simply refrain from patronizing these stores and manufacturers; but actually write to them. Let them know that you cannot, in good conscience, spend your money at their outlets unless they break ties with the pornography they are selling.

National boycotts have been effective tools with network television also. Let the networks know, either by letter or phone call, which shows offend you. Those who control what is being seen on the television screen may not be concerned at all about your morals, but they need you and thousands like you as viewers if they expect to keep ratings high enough to draw sufficient advertising dollars.

Those who have thrown off moral restraint have misused the First Amendment's protection of free speech to justify the production and sale of even the most vile and violent pornography to anyone who wants it — anywhere and at any time. But we do not have to bend to their demands. We can take action to eradicate pornography from our communities. The fight against pornography is really a community fight. By exercising your rights within the guidelines of the First Amendment, your community could be one of those that rises up and halts the flow of filth inside its borders.

Q What can I do to help stop pornography in my community?

A There are several ways in which you can work to remove pornography from your community. One example of how a community has aggressively fought against pornography is of a local church located in the downtown business district of Rome, Georgia. The First Presbyterian Church of Rome successfully intervened in a battle over a city ordinance which restricts the location of adult entertainment establishments, such as nude dance clubs. The local ordinance prohibits these establishments from opening within 500 feet of churches, schools, and residences. A man hoping to start a nude dance club challenged the ordinance by attempting to start his nude dancing club less than 200 feet from the Church. [25] The Church garnered much local support and by intervening made itself a defendant in the suit in order to protect the morals of the community from being debased by such activities as a nude dance club. Rather than staying in the background, the First Presbyterian Church joined the battle on the front lines.

After several months of legal battles, the owner of the proposed nude dance club dismissed his lawsuit against the City of Rome and the First Presbyterian Church. One of the reasons he gave for dropping his lawsuit was that he was not willing to fight against a local church. The presence of the church was central in the decision of the nude dance club owner. Churches across the country should take notice of the power they have when they stand up for what they believe.

Another way to help stop pornography in your community is to work with local city or county commissioners to enact ordinances that restrict the options given to people setting up sexually oriented businesses, such as nude dance clubs or X-rated theaters.

In order to enact such an ordinance government officials must follow several important procedures. First, it must be remembered that currently a municipality can only limit the areas where this type of speech can occur. [26] We cannot enact ordinances that leave no place for these activities, no matter how offensive we may find them. There are several areas of the community that can be kept closed to sexually oriented businesses. Churches, schools, public parks, and residential areas can be set apart in several ways. A local ordinance can establish what is called "set back" provisions. These provisions state that sexually oriented businesses cannot locate within 1,000 feet of a church, a school, a public park, or a residence. A local ordinance could set up specific business zones in which to locate any and all of the sexually oriented businesses.

A city must evaluate the secondary effects of sexually oriented businesses on the community. This does not require that municipalities conduct their own studies. It is enough for municipalities to rely on studies from other cities, as long as those studies are reasonably relied on by the officials enacting the ordinance. [27] We currently have a study being prepared which will enable smaller communities to evaluate the secondary effects of sexually oriented businesses.

When these steps are followed, municipalities can enact ordinances to, at the very least, control where these sexually oriented businesses are located. In addition to the above ideas it is possible for municipalities to control the sale of alcohol at sexually oriented businesses. This can be done by enacting ordinances that limit or control the sale of alcohol at sexually oriented businesses such as nude dance clubs.

Section Three

STUDENTS' RIGHTS OF FREE SPEECH

Chapter One
Rights On Campus

The Supreme Court has consistently upheld the rights of students to express themselves on public school campuses. In 1969 the Supreme Court held that students have the right to speak and express themselves on campus. Then in 1990, in the *Westside Community Board of Education v. Mergens* decision, the Court held that Bible clubs and prayer groups can meet on public secondary school campuses. This case interpreted the Equal Access Act which Congress passed in 1984 to insure that high school students were not discriminated against in the public schools because of their religious beliefs. The following is a brief look at what the Supreme Court decision means to the American Christian student.

The Supreme Court's decision in *Mergens* is a chance for students to share the Gospel with their peers. It is also a sign of the times. Changes are occurring around us daily. The Gospel cannot be stopped. This Supreme Court decision is an answer to the prayers of God's people across our nation and around our world. This 8-1 decision is a clear message to the country that the time is ripe for action.

The American Center for Law and Justice receives thousands of inquiries concerning students' rights in public schools. What follows is a brief response to the most commonly asked questions:

Q What does a Supreme Court decision mean?

A A Supreme Court decision has several meanings in our system of government. The one we are concerned with is the decision's effect on our laws as they affect our public high schools. A decision is binding on all lower courts, both federal and state. This means that they must follow the Supreme Court ruling when the facts are similar. There is no appeal from the Supreme Court. When the Supreme Court rules in a case it becomes the law of the land.

Q Does the Constitution actually require that the "separation of church and state" keeps religion out of the public schools?

A No! First, the Constitution never mentions the phrase "separation of church and state." That phrase was first used by Thomas Jefferson in an address to the Danbury Baptist Association in 1802, 13 years after the Constitution was written and accepted as the law of the United States. Neither is the phrase recorded in the notes of the Constitutional Convention. The constitution does say: "Congress shall make no law respecting an establishment of religion, or prohibiting the free exercise thereof[.]" In fact, the Court has said, on numerous occasions, that separation is impossible. Therefore, the Constitution does not demand that religion be kept out of our public schools. The Constitution only prohibits school-sponsored religious activities. Free Exercise of Religion is our right under the Constitution.

Q What did the Supreme Court say in the Mergens Bible Club Case?

A In the Mergens Bible Club case, the Supreme Court ruled that public secondary schools that receive federal funds and allow noncurriculum related clubs to meet on campus must also allow Bible clubs (Bible clubs also includes prayer groups) to meet on campus during non-instructional time. As Justice O'Connor held speaking for the Court in *Mergens*, "[I]f a State refused to let religious groups use facilities open to others, then it would demonstrate not neutrality but hostility toward religion."[28] The way that our educational system is set up, almost all public secondary schools receive federal funds. This means that if the school has clubs that are allowed to meet on campus that are not a part of a class that is being taught, or are not directly related to a school class, then the school must allow your Bible club the same privilege. In other words, the school must give the Bible club or prayer group official recognition on campus. If the school allows service type clubs, such as Interact, Zonta, or 4-H, or clubs like a chess club, it must allow Bible clubs.

Q Can the Bible Club advertise on campus?

A Yes! Once the Bible club is officially recognized it must be allowed to use the public address system, the school bulletin boards, the school newspaper, and take part in club fairs. Thus, the students can use any form of media available to the other clubs to get the message to the rest of the school.

Q Does this mean that students can now start or attend a Bible club in their public school?

A Yes! The Supreme Court has opened the door for **student - initiated** Bible clubs. The church cannot enter the school and start an outreach program.

Students, however, can now begin their own Christian clubs which have any agenda the students desire. The schools must allow students the freedom to actually start or attend their own meetings on the high school campus where the student attends school.

Q Did the Supreme Court limit the rights of Bible clubs in any way?

A No! The Supreme Court did not limit the rights of Bible clubs in any way. Bible clubs must be treated like any other club in the school with full rights and privileges. The school cannot limit the Bible club in any way. The Bible clubs must be allowed to meet either before school or after school or during a club period with any other clubs. The clubs have a right not only to meet,

48

but also to reach other students with the message that the Bible clubs are meeting.

Q Are the rights of public high school students limited on campus?

A The public high school's mission is to educate students so that they can become productive members of our society. When students do not disrupt the mission of the school they have the same rights as other citizens of the United States. Students even have the right to discuss religion during class time, when religion is a relevant topic. Student behavior that is not illegal or disruptive cannot be stopped by the schools simply because the particular message is offensive to school officials.

Q Can students bring their Bibles to school or wear a Christian shirt?

A Yes! There is no law that prohibits a student from bringing a Bible on campus with him. The student is only bound by an obligation not to "materially or substantially disrupt school discipline."[29] If the student brings his Bible or wears his Christian shirt, the school cannot force the student to remove the shirt or the Bible. Shirts with a message are a form of free speech protected by the First Amendment. *Mergens* clarifies that student speech cannot be discriminated against on campus because of its content.

Q Can public school students share their faith on their campus?

A Yes! In *Mergens*, the Court reinforced students'

rights to evangelize on the high school campus. When we combine *Mergens* with *Tinker v. Des Moines* we find that students' rights are fully protected. Now students can express their First Amendment rights and enjoy the freedom of religion on high school campuses across the country. School officials do not have the right to control student speech just because the particular speech is religious in nature. Students have the right to pass out papers and tracts that are Christian to their peers on campus. As long as the students do not disrupt school discipline, school officials must allow them to be student evangelists. It was argued that to allow the students to meet on campus and to act as student evangelists would violate the Establishment Clause of the First Amendment.

This argument was rejected by the Court in *Mergens*. Thus, *Mergens* is a great victory for Christian high school students in America. With the decision in *Mergens*, the Supreme Court has sent a clear message to the school systems of America. No longer will religious discrimination be tolerated under the guise of "separation of church and state."

Q What about the rights of junior high school students on their campuses?

A This is one of our most frequently asked questions. Junior High School students have the right to pray and have religious discussions on their campus with their peers. They can distribute literature with some restrictions. (see below.) Junior High School students can wear religious t-shirts to school. In addition, junior high school students are covered by the Guidelines which were issued by the Department of Education and discussed below.

The Eighth Circuit Court of Appeals recently upheld the right of junior high school students to form religious clubs on their campuses, when other groups are also meeting. [30] It should be noted that clubs, such as the Boy Scouts, were permitted to meet on school property after school hours. Finding that age was not necessarily a valid reason for discrimination, the Court stated that "the age of the junior high school students does not create an Establishment Clause violation." [31] The Court of Appeals justified its decision by looking at the private nature of the language involved in student clubs when it stated that "[t]here is a crucial difference between government speech endorsing religion, which the Establishment Clause forbids, and private speech endorsing religion, which the Free Speech and Free Exercise Clauses protect." [32]

Furthermore, the Court found that "nothing in the First Amendment postpones the right of religious speech until high school, or draws a line between daylight and evening hours." [33] In the Eighth Circuit, junior high school students have a First Amendment right to use facilities for Bible club meetings when those facilities are being used by other student groups. To our knowledge, no other court has specifically addressed the rights of junior high school students to initiate and attend Bible clubs on their campuses. The court's decision in *Good*

News/Good Sports does, however, set out a thoughtful analysis of why junior high school students should not be discriminated against because of their religious beliefs or their age.

Q What rights do college students have on their campuses?

A This is another frequently asked question. For the present it should suffice for us to say that all of the rights we have discussed in this booklet concerning high school and junior high school students are equally applicable to college students. In fact, the rights of college students are even greater than those of high school students. Future editions of this booklet will include an entirely separate section dealing with the rights of college students.

In a case just decided by the Supreme Court, the University of Virginia authorized payments from a Student Activities Fund for the printing costs of a variety of publications written by student groups. [34] The University prohibited funding of any student publication that "primarily promotes or manifests a particular belief in or about a deity or an ultimate reality." [35] When a Christian newspaper applied for funding, University officials denied the request because of the newspaper's religious viewpoint. School officials were troubled by the mission of the Christian newpaper, which was "to challenge Christians to live, in word and deed, according to the faith they proclaim and to encourage students to consider what a personal relationship with Jesus Christ means." [36]

In response to school officials' arguments that they had a shortage of available funds, the Court stated that "[t]he government cannot justify viewpoint discrimination among private speakers on the economic fact of scarcity. Had the meeting rooms in *Lamb's Chapel* been scarce . . . our decision would have been no different."[37] The Court further stated that the treatment of religion must be neutral when dealing with government programs. "We have held that the guarantee of neutrality is respected, not offended, when the government, following neutral criteria and evenhanded policies, extends benefits to recipients whose ideologies and viewpoints, including religious ones, are broad and diverse."[38] Ultimately, the Supreme Court reversed the decision of the Court of Appeals and allowed the funding of the Christian newspaper at the University. Thus,

even in issues of indirect public funding, it is unconstitutional for government officials to discriminate solely on the basis of a student or a student group's religious beliefs. Indirect public funding would include money from the student activity fund. This means that even Christian groups must be permitted to use funds from the student activity fees, if other student groups are being permitted to use those funds.

Q What rights do I have on campus during the school day?

A In *Tinker*, the Supreme Court held that "students [do not] shed their constitutional rights to freedom of speech or expression at the schoolhouse gate."[39] This means that students have the right to express their religious beliefs during the school day. "When [a student] is in the cafeteria, or on the playing field, or on the campus during the authorized hours, he may express his opinions." [40] If school officials refuse to allow you to pray on campus they are censoring your speech and denying your constitutional rights.

Tinker held that students retain their First Amendment rights when they are rightfully on a public school campus. The one limitation the Court placed on the rights of the students is simple: students must not "materially or substantially disrupt school discipline." [41] Thus, as long as students do not disrupt the school they have the right to pray on campus, even around the flagpole.

The nature of public schools does not justify the forfeiture of constitutional rights. In fact, the nature of public schools should enhance the constitutional rights of students and teachers. The school is to teach the student how the laws of the land apply. What better place for a real-life lesson on freedom of speech and religion?

Q What happens now?

A Now the battle begins. The Court has given Christians the right to gather together in public schools. We must begin to use the right we have been given. If the Supreme Court allows us to meet and we fail to meet, what good comes of the right? Like a muscle, our rights must be exercised or they will disappear again. God has opened up a huge mission field. Our missionaries to this field must be our high school students. They can reach their generation for Jesus. They need your support. Pray that the

Lord will send laborers to work the fields of the harvest in this hour of great need. God has opened a door. We must walk through it!

Q What if my local high school refuses to allow students to meet or hand out literature on their campus in spite of the *Tinker* and *Mergens* decisions?

A The American Center for Law and Justice is undertaking a national campaign to protect students' freedoms of speech, religion and assembly. We are going to make sure that the *Mergens* decision is obeyed by local school boards. We will institute legal proceedings, when appropriate, to ensure the compliance of school boards with the Court's holding in *Mergens*. (Note: see Appendix I for a detailed legal briefing on students' rights.)

Chapter Two
Graduation And Other School Events

Q Can we have student-led prayer at graduation?

A Yes! In *Lee v. Weisman*, the Supreme Court held only that it violates the Establishment Clause for school officials to invite clergy to give prayers at commencement.[42] Justice Kennedy made clear, for the majority, that the Court's decision was limited to the particular facts before the Court.[43] Thus, any change from the factual situation presented in *Lee* might alter the resulting opinion from the Court.

Indeed, following *Lee*, at least one Federal Appeals Court has ruled that "a majority of students can do what the

State acting on its own cannot do to incorporate prayer in public high school graduation ceremonies." [44] In *Jones v. Clear Creek Independent School District* (*Jones*), a post-*Lee* decision, the Fifth Circuit upheld the constitutionality of a school district resolution permitting high school seniors to include a student-led invocation in their graduation ceremony if the majority of the class so votes. [45] Quite unlike the school-directed and school-controlled practice found unconstitutional in *Lee*, the Clear Creek Independent School District's resolution simply permits the students of each graduating class to decide if they do or do not wish to have an invocation as a part of their commencement. In the event that students choose to include an invocation, the resolution provides that it shall be nonsectarian and nonproselytizing and conducted only by a student volunteer.

The *Jones II* Court recognized, as the Supreme Court has previously held, that "there is a crucial difference between government speech endorsing religion, which the Establishment Clause forbids, and private speech endorsing religion, which the Free Speech and Free Exercise Clauses protect." [46]

The Fifth Circuit is the only United States Court of Appeals to have addressed the rights of students to initiate prayers at graduation following the Supreme Court's decision in *Lee v. Weisman*. On June 7, 1993, the Supreme Court denied certiorari in *Jones II*. In other words, the Supreme Court let stand the Fifth Circuit Court of Appeals' decision permitting student-initiated prayer at graduation. Thus, the Fifth Circuit's opinion in *Jones II* provides school boards across the nation, both in and outside the Fifth Circuit, with a valid legal basis for choosing to uphold the rights of students to initiate prayers at graduation. [47]

In *Harris v. Joint School District*, [48] the Court of Appeals decided that prayer during a high school graduation ceremony violated the Establishment Clause. This decision directly conflicted with the Fifth Circuit's opinion in *Jones v. Clear Creek*, which upheld the right of students to conduct prayer at graduation ceremonies. In the 1994-95 term the Supreme Court granted review in *Harris* and vacated the Court of Appeals decision as moot — because a viable claim no longer exists. This ruling by the Supreme Court leaves *Jones v. Clear Creek* as the only federal appeals court decision on the issue of student-led graduation prayer.

Some may suggest that school officials should aggressively censor all student expression simply because it occurs within the jurisdiction of the school. The law regarding the First Amendment rights of students, however, is well-established. Student speech cannot be restricted because of the content of that speech.

Q Can valedictorians, salutatorians, or honorary student speakers give speeches on religious subjects, including reading from the Bible?

A Yes! As stated previously, it is well settled that religious speech is protected by the First Amendment of the

Constitution. [49] The Supreme Court has firmly held that school administrators can only prohibit protected speech by students when it "materially and substantially interfere[s] with the requirements of appropriate discipline in the operation of the school." [50]

Where students have been granted freedom to compose their own speeches (e.g., valedictorian or salutatorian addresses, etc.), or even their own commencement exercise, protected student expression should not be subjected to censorship because of its content. In fact, it is a fundamental proposition of constitutional law that a governmental body may not suppress or exclude the speech of private parties for the sole reason that the speech contains a religious perspective. [51] To deny this bedrock principle would be to undermine the essential guarantees of free speech and religious freedom under the First Amendment.

There is quite a difference between refusing to direct prayer or invite clergy to give prayer at graduation, and choosing to prohibit individual student expression based on its content. The First Amendment precludes any governmental effort to single out and censor - or otherwise burden - the speech of private parties solely because that speech is religious. [52]

A decision by a school board to respect the free speech rights of students and to refrain from censoring student speech based solely on its content is not a deliberate violation of the law. As the Supreme Court has emphasized, students' free speech rights apply even "when [a student] is in the cafeteria, or on the playing field, or on campus during authorized hours . . . ." [53] Students do not "shed their constitutional rights to freedom of speech or expression at the schoolhouse gate". [54] The same axiom is true at graduation.

Q Can we have Baccalaureate services?

A Yes! Students, community groups and area churches are entitled to sponsor events, such as baccalaureate services. If school facilities are available to the community for use, these groups must be allowed to use school facilities also, regardless of the religious nature of their activities. A policy of equal access for religious speech conveys a message "of neutrality rather than endorsement; if a State refused to let religious groups use facilities open to others, then it would demonstrate not neutrality but hostility toward religion." [55] The United States District Court for the District of Wyoming recently issued a preliminary injunction which allowed a baccalaureate service in a public high school. The court relied directly on *Lamb's Chapel.* [56]

Q Are official "Moments of Silence" permissible under current law?

A Yes! The Supreme Court reviewed the issue of official, "moments of silence" in *Wallace v. Jaffree.* [57] While it is true that the Supreme Court did find the particular "moment of silence" statute before the Court in that case unconstitutional, the *Wallace* Court did not declare that all "moments of silence" violate the Establishment Clause. In fact, a majority of the

Wallace Court clearly recognized that moments of silence are constitutionally permissible: "I agree fully with Justice O'Connor's assertion that some moment-of-silence statutes may be constitutional, a suggestion set forth in the Court's opinion as well." [58] Furthermore, all parties in the *Wallace* case agreed that an Alabama statute mandating a "moment of silence" during class time was constitutional. [59] *Wallace* held only that the particular facts of the case made the Alabama statute calling for a moment of silence "for meditation or voluntary prayer"during class time unconstitutional. [60] Specifically, the Court focused on the clearly religious intent expressed by the statute's sponsors in the recorded legislative history, and the express language of the statute which called for a moment of silence "for meditation or voluntary prayer." [61]

After *Wallace*, it is clear that any official moment of silence must be motivated by a well-defined secular purpose and be neutral on its face, leaving the use of the "moment of silence" to individuals and the dictates of their own consciences.

Q Do students have a right to pray together at school and participate in events like the See You at the Pole National Day of Prayer?

A Yes! See You at the Pole National Day of Prayer is a student-led and student-initiated event. On an annual basis, students across the nation gather with like-minded peers around the flagpole at their respective schools before the class day begins and pray for their schools, teachers, administrators and country.

As discussed in earlier sections, students retain their constitutional rights of free speech and expression, including the right to pray and share personal beliefs, while on their public school campuses. Under the *Tinker* standard, school officials may restrict protected student speech only if it "materially and substantially interfere[s] with appropriate discipline." [62] Thus, school officials may not prevent students from gathering together for prayer and religious discussion on school grounds, provided that students do so in a non-disruptive manner during non-instructional time. Non-instructional time would be immediately before and after school, at lunchtime, or any other "free" time when students are permitted to talk and mingle with peers on campus.

It should be noted that while school officials may not prevent students from engaging in protected religious expression unless it "materially and substantially interferes with school discipline," [63] they may impose reasonable time, place and manner restrictions. Such restrictions, however, must be content neutral, "narrowly tailored to serve a significant government interest, and leave open ample alternative channels of communication." [64]

Q Can a See You At The Pole rally be held even if it is not part of an officially recognized club on campus?

A Yes! *Tinker* stands for students' rights to freedom of speech and expression. As long as the activity being participated in does

61

not "materially or substantially interfere with school discipline" students have the right to gather together on campus for prayer, even if no prayer group or Bible club is officially recognized on their campus.

Prayer is a protected form of speech that cannot be banned by school officials when it is being offered in a manner such as See You At The Pole. School officials refusing students the right to pray on their campus is nothing short of censorship.

If there is an officially recognized Bible Club or Prayer Group on campus, then students in the club can advertise the Prayer Rally. Students must be allowed to use the same forms of advertisement that the other clubs are allowed to use. That includes the public address system, the school bulletin boards, and the school newspaper.

Q Is it constitutional to have holiday observances, in the public schools?

A Yes! Students, of course, are free to express their beliefs and convictions as they apply to particular holidays, provided they do so in a non-disruptive manner. (See the discussion of students' rights and *Tinker*, above and in Appendix I.) For example, students have the right to distribute Christmas cards or religious tracts on the "true meaning of Christmas" to their peers during non-instructional time. Students could also wish their classmates a "Merry Christmas" or a "Happy Hanukkah." School officials could not constitutionally prohibit such activities. Further, students may express their individual beliefs during classroom discussions, as well as in the context of appropriate class assignments. For instance, an elementary student when instructed to draw a "Thanksgiving" picture may choose to draw a picture of a pilgrim praying to God. Or, when told to prepare an essay on a topic of choice, a student may select the birth of Christ, or any other religious topic the student wishes. School officials cannot discriminate against a student's work simply because of its religious nature.

Regarding official public school observance of religious holidays, an issue separate and distinct from protected student expression, the Eighth Circuit has held that religious songs and symbols can be used in the public schools if they are presented in a "prudent and objective manner and only as part of the cultural and religious heritage of the holiday." [65] The *Florey* Court also stated that the study and performance of religious songs is constitutional if the purpose is the "advancement of the students' knowledge of society's cultural and religious heritage, as well as the provision of an opportunity for students to perform a full range of music, poetry, and drama that is likely to be of interest to the students and their audience." [66]

The *Florey* decision was based largely on a United States Supreme Court opinion: School *District of Abington Township v. Schempp.* [67] In *Schempp*, the Supreme Court said, "It certainly may be said that the Bible is worthy of study for its literary and historic qualities. Nothing we have said here indicates that such study of the Bible or of religion, when presented objectively as part of a secular program of education, may not be effected consistently with the First Amendment." [68]

Q Can the Bible be used as part of the curriculum of the school?

A Yes! In *Stone v. Graham*, the Supreme Court said, "the Bible may constitutionally be used in an appropriate study of history, civilization, ethics, comparative religion, or the like." [69] Thus, it would be constitutional for a public school teacher to have students study the biblical passages that relate to Christmas (e.g., Matthew 1:18-2:22 and Luke 2:1-20) if the purpose was to study the historical or literary significance of the passages. Of course, any student that had ideological or religious objections to reading the Bible should be excused from the assignment.

In addition, the Bible was an important book in the early history of this country. It is possible to set up a curriculum that evaluates the role of the Bible in this country and western civilization that is constitutional. The Bible is also considered to be literature from antiquity. A school board could establish a policy that allows the Bible to be discussed as part of a literature program in the school.

Q Can members of the community or organizations use school facilities for religious purposes?

A Yes! Members of the local community also have free speech rights in the school if the district rents school facilities to outsiders during non-school hours. In other words, if the school district rents its facilities to non-school groups during non-school hours, then the school district has a constitutional duty to rent to religious speakers, such as a local church that wants to rent a facility for its annual Christmas pageant. [70]

The Supreme Court recently rejected an exclusion of religious speakers from public schools in *Lamb's Chapel*. In refusing to uphold a religious exclusion, the *Lamb's Chapel* Court stated that "the principle that has emerged from our cases is that the First Amendment forbids the government to regulate speech in ways that favor some viewpoints or ideas at the expense of others." [71] The *Lamb's Chapel* decision reinforces the rights of religious persons to express their views publicly.

Q Can Christmas vacation still be called Christmas vacation?

A Yes! Finally, school districts are under no constitutional obligation to rename "Christmas vacation" as "Winter vacation" or some similar name. Any suggestion to the contrary is simply unnecessary and should be avoided. The Supreme Court itself has acknowledged with approval that Congress gives federal employees a paid holiday on December 25 and that Congress calls it, "Christmas." [72]

Chapter Three

Opting Out Of Objectionable Classes

We live in a society where the state mandates that children attend school. Most American students attend public schools. Public schools teach a curriculum that has been required by the State Board of Education and the local school board. Educational theories change from time to time. When those changes occur, there is a period of time when school officials try out new ideas in an attempt to find the best way to convey the knowledge to the students. One of the problems with this concept is that experimental ideas are often on the edge of what is acceptable to society. When they are implemented, parents often find their children being taught ideas that are objectionable to family beliefs.

In the past, parents had very few options when their children faced instruction from school officials that was out of step with what the family believed. Many of the families affected by this particular problem were religious, often Christian.

While parents may have little direct say about what ends up in public school curricula, federal law has given parents clear rights to exempt their children from experimental or values-related classes that depart from academics. The Hatch Amendment (passed in 1984) was designed to reinforce parental control of their children's education. Based on the Hatch Amendment, parents may have their child excluded from experimental programs.

The Hatch Amendment, also known as the Pupil Rights Amendment, says parents have the right to inspect all instructional material, including that used in experimental or testing programs. Unless parental consent is given, no student shall be required to submit to any kind of test designed to reveal information concerning political affiliations, potentially embarrassing psychological problems, sexual behavior and attitudes, illegal and anti-social behavior, critical appraisals of family relationships, legally privileged relationships (such as those with a minister or doctor), and income.

If your school introduces practices that appear related to the occult, such as visualizing conversations with dead historical figures, chanting a mantra-like slogan, practicing any form of meditation, and so on, then the Establishment Clause of the First Amendment works on your side. The Establishment Clause forbids the state from setting up one religion over and against other religions. Since these practices are religious and state-sponsored, they represent a violation of your rights.

If you even suspect your child may be facing situations like these, attempt to find out immediately what is happening. Do not wait for your child to come home with horror stories halfway through the school year with much of the damage already done. Any sex education course or anything that appears to be remotely experimental in your child's curriculum needs thorough investigation right away. Check the materials. Meet the teacher. Question your children from day one. Whenever possible personally monitor the classes so you know week-in and week-out what your child is being taught.

Furthermore, stay in constant touch with your children about the content and teaching methods of what appear to be routine classes. A teacher can insert an unorthodox bias — whether it is amoral, anti-Christian, anti-family, anti-life, or anti-American - into any class in a potent way. Be sensitive to this possibility by staying in close contact with your child, the school and your child's teachers.

If your school system is beginning to introduce a sex education course, get involved. Lobby the school board or its designated committee to consider a traditional sex curriculum, such as Teen-Aid or Project Respect. [73] Any proper sex education course should teach abstinence as the primary and normal method of birth control prior to marriage. You will have to fight the charge that such an approach is unrealistic among today's licentious teenagers. Do not give in to such defeatist logic.

If your school system already integrates liberal sex educators such as Planned Parenthood or homosexual advocates such as California's Project 10, you probably have grounds to object. Such programs usually cross over from objective teaching to advocating amorality. Appeal to your school board that the course undermines parental authority by implying to students that everyone their age is having sex, or by teaching that homosexuality is normal, or by telling students that they can easily and confidentially arrange abortions without their parents' knowledge. A religion can be any set of beliefs by which a person lives and trains their children to live, even amorality. If necessary, object on First Amendment grounds. Show that the state is illegally establishing a religion by advocating amorality.

As a more immediate tactic, find out when the outside sex program representative will be speaking to classes. Get concerned parents to take turns sitting in on classroom discussions. Planned Parenthood has been known to tidy up its presentations when parents are present.

You should try to resolve any such objectionable classroom practices locally. Appeal to the teacher, then the principal, then the school board. If those appeals fail, and you are dealing with a clear example of a school trying to implement a New Age practice, legal action could prove successful on a First Amendment basis. If appeals fail regarding values clarification or any sort of classroom therapy, the Hatch Amendment provides grounds for appeal through the U.S. Department of Education. Remember, this law does not prohibit the course, but it does prohibit your child from being included without your permission.

You can formally request that the school inform you of questionable educational materials and practices.

Do not be intimidated by the objection that a certain course falls outside the law because it was not developed with federal funds. The burden of proof is on the school to prove that the course used absolutely no tax money in its development, and this is unlikely. Any complaints you make should state all details of the violation. They can be filed through the Family Educational Rights and Privacy Act Office, U.S. Department of Education, 400 Maryland Ave. S.W., Washington, D.C. 20202.

Section Four

UNITED STATES DEPT. OF EDUCATION DIRECTIVES TO ALL SUPERINTENDENTS

In a recent speech

before high school students in Virginia, President Bill Clinton came out in favor of religious speech in our nation's public schools. He emphasized the need for us to continue to be a nation of toleration for the beliefs of others. He also discussed the need for us to no longer disqualify students simply because of their religious beliefs.

President Clinton specifically addressed the rights of students to express their beliefs on campus. He stated that students have the right to "pray privately and individually whenever they want. They can say grace themselves before lunch. There are times when they can pray out loud together. Student religious clubs in high schools can and should be treated just like any other extracurricular club. They can advertise their meetings, meet on school grounds, use school facilities just as other clubs can. When students can choose to read a book to themselves, they have every right to read the Bible or any other religious text they want."

In continuing to address the rights of students, President Clinton stated, "[s]tudents should feel free to express their religion and their beliefs in homework, through their work, during class presentations. . . . If students can distribute flyers or pamphlets that have nothing to do with the school, they can distribute religious flyers and pamphlets. . . . If students can wear T-shirts advertising sports teams, rock groups or politicians, they can also wear T-shirts that promote religion."

He declared the need for the government to protect the rights of students by noting that "some student religious groups haven't been allowed to publicize their meetings in the same way that nonreligious groups can. Some students have been prevented even from saying grace before lunch." The President then offered solutions to the problem of religious discrimination: "[w]herever and whenever the religious rights of children are threatened or suppressed, **we must move quickly to correct it. We want to make it easier and more acceptable for people to express and to celebrate their faith.**"

President Clinton has even given the Justice Department guidelines for implementing his stated religious rights on public school campuses. The heart of the President's speech is summed up in this one statement taken from the speech: "This country needs to be a place where religion grows and flourishes."

The President's Guidelines were distributed to every public school superintendent in the country at the beginning of the 1995-96 school year by Richard W. Riley, the Secretary of Education for the United States. These Guidelines specify the rights of students on their public school campuses.

Q What are the Directives concerning establishing a Bible Club on public school campuses?

A The Guidelines have a separate section concerning the Equal Access Act, which established the right of secondary school students to have Bible Clubs on their campus. Here is what the Guidelines set out as the United States Department of Education's interpretation of the Equal Access Act:

Student religious groups at public

secondary schools have the same right of access to school facilities as is enjoyed by other comparable student groups. [74]

Schools that meet the requirements of the Equal Access Act "may not refuse access to student religious groups." [75]

A meeting may include a prayer service, Bible reading, or other worship exercise. [76]

A school "must allow student groups meeting under the Act to use the school media — including **the public address system, the school newspaper, and the school bulletin board** — to announce their meetings on the same terms as other noncurriculum-related student groups are allowed to use the school media." [77]

Finally, a school creates a limited open forum under the Equal Access Act, triggering equal access rights for religious groups, when it allows students to meet during their **lunch periods** or **other noninstructional** time during the school day, as well as when it allows students to meet before and after the school day. [78] (Emphasis added.)

Thus, the Guidelines basically restate the law as addressed in the main body of this booklet.

Q What do the Guidelines say regarding student prayer and religious discussion?

A The Guidelines address the issue of a student's right to pray, or generally participate in religious discussion on campus. In a nutshell, students have the right to pray, or have religious discussions, during the school day provided that students do so in a non-disruptive manner. These rights include the right to "persuade, their peers." [79]

The Establishment Clause of the First Amendment does not prohibit purely private religious speech by students. Students, therefore, have the same right to engage in individual or group prayer and religious discussion during the school day as they do to engage in other comparable activity. For example, **students may read their Bibles** or other scriptures, **say grace before meals**, and **pray before tests** to the same extent they may engage in comparable non-disruptive activities. Local school authorities . . . may **not** structure or administer such rules to discriminate against religious activity or speech. [80] (Emphasis added.)

The Guidelines then get even more specific about the rights of students to pray on their campuses:

[S]tudents in informal settings, such as cafeterias and hallways, may pray and discuss their religious views with each other. . . Students may also speak to, and **attempt to persuade, their peers** about religious topics. . . . [81]

Clearly students have the right to pray and have religious discussions with their peers on their campuses, including the right to evangelize or persuade their peers.

Q Do the Guidelines discuss rallies like the annual See You At The Pole rally?

A Yes. The Guidelines specifically address the right of students to gather on their campuses for events such as See You At The Pole. The Guidelines make it very clear that such events are considered to be constitutional. While school officials should remain neutral on the issue of student religious speech:

> Students may . . . participate in before or after school events with religious content, such as "see you at the flag pole" (sic). . . gatherings. [82]

Q Do the Guidelines address the issue of prayer at graduation ceremonies and baccalaureate ceremonies?

A Yes and No. The Guidelines offer no direction regarding graduation prayer. What has been discussed earlier in this supplement and in the original book is a good explanation of the law concerning students' rights to pray at graduation.

The Guidelines do affirm the rights of students as to baccalaureate services.

> If a school generally opens its facilities to private groups, it must make its facilities available on the same terms to organizers of privately sponsored religious baccalaureate services. [83]

In short, baccalaureate services can take place on campus as long as they are privately sponsored and the school facilities are open for the use of outside organizations during non-school hours.

Q According to the Guidelines, is it constitutional to teach about religion in a public school?

A Yes. Schools may teach about religion, even when such teaching includes the use of the Bible. It must be remembered that school officials should be careful not to actually teach religion in such a manner that endorses a particular religious belief. Even though school officials cannot endorse religious beliefs they may teach the history of religion, comparative religion, the Bible-as-literature, and the role of religion in the history of the United States and other countries. [84] In addition, it is permissible to consider religious influences on art, music, literature, and social studies. [85] Public school officials may also teach about religious holidays and even celebrate the secular aspects of those holidays as long as they do not observe these holidays as religious events or promote such observance by students. [86]

Q What do the Guidelines say about student assignments?

A The First Amendment protects student rights, including the right of students to express their religious beliefs in their school work. School officials must not discriminate against a student due to the religious content of a particular student's assignment.

Students may express their beliefs about religion in the form of homework, artwork, and other written and oral assignments free of discrimination based on the religious content of their submissions. [87]

Therefore, students are free to express their religious beliefs in their homework or classwork, as long as the religious beliefs expressed are relevant to the particular assignment.

Q Can students distribute religious literature to their schoolmates?

A Yes. The Guidelines specifically address the rights of students to distribute religious literature on their public school campuses. While there are some limitations on the right of students to hand their schoolmates religious literature, it is important to understand that school officials cannot discriminate against students solely because of the religious nature of their literature.

School officials may regulate the time, place, and manner of literature distribution as long as they have the same rules for all students regardless of their religious beliefs. **School officials may not single out religious literature for special regulation**. [88/89]

The Guidelines are very clear concerning literature distribution:

Students have a right to distribute religious literature to their schoolmates on the same terms as they are permitted to distribute other literature that is unrelated to school curriculum or activities. Schools may impose the same reasonable time, place, and manner or other constitutional restrictions on distribution of religious literature as they do on non-school literature generally, but **they may not single out religious literature for special regulation**. [90]

(Emphasis added.)

Q What do the Guidelines say about religious excusals and release time for off-campus religious instruction?

A These two issues are ultimately controlled by state law. If state law permits excusals, then school officials are permitted to allow students to be excused from an assignment that is objectionable to the student or the student's parents on religious or other conscientious grounds. In the same manner, the Guidelines state that release time is also constitutional. [91] Release time is a program where students are permitted to leave campus and go to another location for the sole purpose of receiving religious instruction.

In both of these examples, school officials must be careful not to encourage or discourage students to take advantage of these rights. Thus, school officials can neither reward nor punish students who do or do not participate in these rights. [92]

Q Do the Guidelines address the issue of teaching values in public schools?
A Yes. School officials are permitted to teach "civic values and virtue, and the moral code that holds us together as a community." [93] Because school officials are government employees there are potential problems if school officials do not remain neutral with respect to religion. Neutral means that a school official can neither support, nor oppose religion, in teaching values in public schools.

It is important to note that some of the values which will be taught are religious; however, that does not make it unlawful to teach them in school. This is again a concept of neutrality. The fact that it is considered immoral to commit a murder does not become a value that is unteachable because the Bible commands Christians not to murder.

Q What about wearing clothing with religious messages?

A Students have the right to wear t-shirts and other clothing with religious messages on them. The Guidelines explain the right of students to wear what the Guidelines refer to as "student garb" with a religious message. The key factor to be considered is that **"[r]eligious messages may not be singled out for suppression."** [94]

Students may display religious messages on items of clothing to the same extent that they are permitted to display other comparable messages. [95]

What this means is simple. If t-shirts are permitted by school officials, there cannot be a requirement that forbids the wearing of t-shirts with religious messages. Furthermore, items such as yarmulkes and head scarves generally may not be prohibited by school officials. [96]

Students have the right to express their religious beliefs through the clothing they wear. It should be noted, however, that school officials may from time to time prohibit certain t-shirts. An example of this is the t-shirt that depicts violence. If such a shirt has been prohibited it is possible that a Christian shirt that has blood on it will also be prohibited. The important concept to remember is that if only the Christian shirt is being prohibited it is likely that some form of religious discrimination is occurring.

Conclusion The Department of Education Directives should help to clear up some areas of law that are important to Christians. It is my hope that the Directives will help ensure that Christian students are no longer treated like second-class citizens. I believe that the Directives will help students to realize that they have the right to evangelize on their campuses, in a non-disruptive manner, during the school day.

By issuing the Guidelines, the Department of Education has reinforced the rights of students across America to stand up for what they believe when they are on campus. Clearly, the laws of this country support students' rights to present the Gospel of Jesus Christ to their friends while they are on their public school campuses.

Section Five

CHRISTIAN RIGHTS IN THE WORKPLACE:

Chapter One

Fighting Religious Discrimination

Employee Religious Rights

Q What is Title VII and how does it protect employees?

A The religious freedom of most employees is protected by a federal law called "Title VII".[97] In order to be protected by Title VII, an employee must show that: (1) He holds a sincere religious belief that conflicts with an employment requirement; (2) He has informed the employer about the conflict; and (3) He was discharged, disciplined or subjected to discriminatory treatment for failing to comply with the conflicting employment requirement.[98]

1. Sincerely held religious belief.

The sincerity of

religious belief is rarely at issue in Title VII cases. Although failure to act on a religious belief consistently may be considered evidence that the belief is not sincerely held,[99] the fact that the belief was only recently acquired does not render it an insincere one.[100] An employee is not held "to a standard of conduct which would have discounted his beliefs based on the slightest perceived flaw in the consistency of his religious practice."[101]

Religion under Title VII is broadly defined as including "all aspects of religious observance and practice, as well as belief...."[102] The EEOC defines religious practices as including "moral or ethical beliefs as to what is right and wrong which are sincerely held with the strength of traditional religious views.... The fact that no religious group espouses such beliefs or the fact that the religious group to which the individual professes to belong may not accept such belief will not determine whether the belief is a religious belief of the employee...."[103] In other words, the EEOC's test does not require that the employee's religious beliefs coincide with the tenets of his church: "Title VII protects more than the observance of Sabbath or practices specifically mandated by an employee's religion...."[104] Religion under Title VII has been held to include the Black Muslim faith, the "old Catholic Religion," a "faith in humanity being," and atheism.[105] However, "religion" has not been so broadly defined as to include membership in the Ku Klux Klan, membership in the United Klans of America, or belief in the spiritual power of a certain cat food.[106]

2. Employee informed employer of religious belief.

Next the employee must show that the employer was aware of the belief. An employer has sufficient notice of an employee's religious belief if he has enough information about the employee's "religious needs to permit the employer to understand the existence of a conflict between employee's religious practices and the employer's job requirements."[107] The best way to inform the employer is in writing. A simple letter to the employer stating: "I have a sincerely held religious belief to (or not to) _____. I am requesting that you, my employer, accommodate this sincerely held religious belief by allowing me to (or not requiring me to) _____." The employee should sign and date the letter, and keep a copy.

Notification in writing is not absolutely necessary, as long as the employer is aware of the beliefs.[108] A written notification however, gives the employer a fair chance to attempt to accommodate your religious convictions by avoiding confusion or disputes over whether they actually had notice.[109]

This requirement must not be ignored. An employee's claim will be rejected if the employer does not understand the religious beliefs involved.[110]

3. Discriminatory treatment of employee.

If an employee can show they have a sincerely held religious belief and that the employer knew about it, Title VII prohibits the employer from discriminating against the employee because of the belief. "Discrimination" includes demotion, layoff, transfer, failure to promote, discharge, harassment, intimidation, or the threat of these adverse employment actions.[111]

The employer is also required to reasonably accommodate the employee's religious beliefs unless such accommodation would result in undue hardship to the employer.[112] "Accommodation" means that employer neutrality is not enough.[113] The employer must take affirmative steps to attempt to eliminate any burden on the employee's religion. In general, an employer is required to accommodate an employee's adherence to the principles of his religion unless such accommodation will actually interfere with the operations of the employer.

Chapter Two

Employees Of Private, Non-Government Organizations

Most employees work for private employers, not for the government. These employees are primarily protected only by Title VII. They may also be protected by laws in their State similar to Title VII. State laws protecting the religious freedom of employees may provide more protection than Title VII, but generally they are very similar to the federal law. This booklet does not attempt to describe individual state laws, therefore employees should consult an attorney who is licensed in their particular state to determine if state law provides them with added protection.

This chapter explains how employees of private organizations are protected by Title VII. The rules of law stated apply to govern-

82

ment employees, but focus on private employees because Title VII is usually their only remedy.

Q Can I share the Gospel with co-workers at work?

A Yes. If required by their religious beliefs, an employee's religiously motivated expressions of faith are protected by Title VII. For instance, in conversations with other employees, you may refer to Biblical passages on slothfulness and "work ethics."[114] Employees can engage in religious speech at work as long as there is no actual imposition on co-workers or disruption of the work routine.[115] Generally, no disruption of the work routine will occur if an employee's witnessing takes place during breaks, or other free time. If other employees are permitted to use electronic mail and screen savers for speech that is not related to work, an employee who has a sincerely held religious belief to communicate their faith with others should also be able to use these modes of communication.

To ensure that their religious speech is protected by Title VII, an employee should first of all be able to honestly say that their religious beliefs require them to share the Gospel whenever possible with willing co-workers during breaks or other free time. The employee must then inform the employer of this religious belief (preferably in writing). At that point, the employer must attempt to accommodate this religious belief unless it will cause the employer "undue hardship."

Q Can I keep my Bible or other religious items at my desk?

A Yes. As with witnessing to co-workers, an employee can bring his Bible to work and keep it at his desk if he is required to do so by sincerely held religious beliefs. To ensure that this religious belief of having a Bible or other religious items at work is protected by Title VII, an employee should first of all be able to honestly say that their religious beliefs require them to bring these items to work. The employee must then inform the employer of this religious belief (preferably in writing). The employer is then required to attempt to accommodate this belief.

Q Is my employer permitted to restrict what I say when I am not at work?

A No. Employers generally cannot discriminate against employees because of religious speech expressed outside of the workplace.[116] The only possible exception is if speech activity engaged in outside the workplace directly affects the employee's ability to perform his job properly.

For instance, even though not acting in their official capacity, judges have been prohibited from speaking out about issues on which they may have to rule.[117]

Q Do I have to work on Sundays if my religion prohibits it?

A Employers must accommodate requests by employees for absence on their Sabbath or other religious holidays. An affirmative duty arises under Title VII for the employer to make a good faith effort to arrange the employee's schedule to allow the employee to have Sabbaths off.[118] The employer will be in violation of Title VII if they have "made no real

84

effort" or have taken a "don't care" attitude.[119]

For instance, courts have held that an employer is required to accommodate a World Wide Church of God employee who observed his Sabbath from sunset on Friday to sunset on Saturday. The reason for this decision is that the employer did not incur additional costs from the accommodation because they employed extra men at all times to cover unscheduled absences. [120]

The employer's affirmative duty to attempt to accommodate the employee's request for time off is not limited if the employee asks for more than one accommodation. For instance, an employee who belongs to the World Wide Church of God requested time off in view of two sincerely held religious beliefs: (1) attending a religious festival during her normal working shift, and (2) refraining from all work during the religious festival. The employer argued that accommodating one of these religious beliefs satisfied their duty under Title VII. But the Court ruled against the employer, refusing to "condone an employer's entire lack of effort to accommodate a given conflict merely because the employer offered to accommodate other ones."[121]

The same rule applies where an employee's religious beliefs prevent him from working on Sundays, and prevent him from asking someone else to engage in this prohibited activity for him. Merely allowing the employee to swap shifts with someone does not constitute reasonable accommodation in this instance. In addition to allowing the employee to be off on Sundays, the employer has an affirmative duty to arrange a swap for the employee. [122] Employees must be careful to specifically inform their employer of this religious belief not to ask anyone else to work on Sunday either.

In sum, employers must attempt to accommodate an employee's need for days off due to religious beliefs. At a minimum, the employer's duty to accommodate includes allowing employees to trade shifts, and may require the employer to arrange for the trade.

Q Can my employer force me to work on jobs that support abortion?

A Title VII requires employers to accommodate employees who refuse to do specific tasks because of a conflict with religious beliefs. For instance, an employer has been required to accommodate a religious worker's objections to abortion. [123] In that case, an Internal Revenue Service employee refused to handle applications for tax exempt status submitted by any organization which supported abortion. The court ruled that accommodating the employee would not result in undue hardship to the employer because the number of applications the employee might refuse to handle would be relatively insignificant as compared to his total workload.

So employees who have a religious objection to abortion can request that their employer not require them to work on projects involving abortion. The employer will be required to grant this request if it can assign these projects to other employees without undue hardship.

Q Can my employer require me to speak in a way that violates

my religious convictions?

A An employee cannot be forced to speak in a manner that would violate his religion. For example, when an employee was fired for refusing, based on religious beliefs, to answer the telephone with "Merry Christmas, Lesco," the court found that the employer should have accommodated the Jehovah's Witness employee's religious convictions regarding the observance of Christmas.[124] The employer should have provided other ways for the employee to answer the phone or assigned her to a different task during the Christmas season.

Q Do I have to pay union dues if it would violate my religious beliefs?

A No. Many employees object to the causes that some unions support, such as Planned Parenthood, or other pro-abortion organizations. Several courts have held that those objecting to the payment of union dues on religious grounds should be accommodated by allowing employees to contribute an amount equal to their dues to an acceptable charity.[125] Another possible accommodation is discounting the union dues in proportion to the amount of money spent on the objectionable union activity.[126]

Q Can I go to work dressed in the particular fashion required by my religion?

A Employers must accommodate religious beliefs requiring an employee to dress or groom in a certain manner, unless the rule prohibiting certain religious garb is justified by a business necessity. The EEOC has ruled that a nurse whose Old Catholic faith required her to wear a scarf was unlawfully discharged for refusing to come to work without the scarf, because requiring the nurse to wear a cap instead of the scarf was "not so necessary to the operation of [the employer's] business as to justify the effect that this policy has upon the religious convictions." [127] Title VII has also been found to protect an employee's religious belief that she must wear a Pro-Life button at all times, even at work. [128]

An employer, however, does not discriminate against an employee by requiring him to shave his long facial hair and refrain from wearing a turban, if both of these religious practices result in safety hazards by preventing a hard hat and respirator from being worn properly. [129]

Q Are there any types of religious beliefs or behavior not protected by Title VII?

A Generally, all sincerely held religious beliefs are protected by Title VII. When a Title VII religious claim fails, it is often because the employer is able to show the employee was discriminated against for inefficiency, bad work product, or an inability to get along with co-workers rather than because of the asserted religious practice. A frequent example is when an employee's religious speech is couched in an argumentative, confrontational style that inhibits cooperation with other employees.[130] In such cases, the court is likely to determine that the employee was not discriminated against because of his religious beliefs, but because of his offensive conduct in the office.[131]

Q Do I have to attend training if it violates my religious convictions?

A An employee cannot be required to attend training that will violate their sincerely held religious beliefs. The EEOC has ruled that an employer violates Title VII if it requires an employee to attend training containing a philosophy that conflicts with the employee's religious beliefs. [132] The EEOC found that the employer failed to show how accommodating the religious convictions of these employees by not requiring them to attend the training would result in an undue hardship.

Q When can my employer refuse to accommodate my religious beliefs because it will cause an undue hardship?

A There are very few times when employers can require employees to violate their religious beliefs, or refuse to allow the employee to practice his religious beliefs at work. Employees can take such actions only if it would cause the employer an undue hardship. In order to successfully assert this defense, courts require that the employer demonstrate attempted accommodation before claiming undue hardship. [133]

Employers must also be able to show evidence of undue hardship that is more than mere speculation.[134] For example, undue hardship requires more than proof that other employees would grumble or be unhappy about a particular accommodation.[135]

"[A]n employer does not sustain his burden of proof merely by showing that an accommodation would be bothersome to administer or disruptive of the operative routine. In addition, ... [courts] are somewhat skeptical of hypothetical hardships that an employer thinks might be caused by an accommodation that never has been put into practice. The employer is on stronger ground when he has attempted various methods of accommodation and can point to hardships that actually resulted."[136]

An employer is not required, however, to accommodate a particular religious belief if it would require more than a de minimis cost. For instance, an employer does not have to accommodate a religious belief to be off on Sundays if it would cause the employer to adjust the seniority policy and pay overtime to a replacement.[137] Employers may also consider public safety when establishing undue hardship. For instance, substituting an untrained employee for a highly trained lineman to work on high-voltage power lines could result in undue hardship.[138]

It should also be emphasized that the Establishment Clause has absolutely no bearing on private employers. At the ACLJ we often hear private employers attempt to justify their discriminatory treatment of religious employees by quoting the phrase "separation of church and state." Even if this phrase were the law, and it is not, it would not require private employees to have religion-free work environments. Private people or companies are not the government and therefore can never violate the Establishment Clause.[139]

Q How do I file a claim under Title VII if my religious rights have been violated?

A It is recommended that the employee contact an attorney before beginning this process. Because the process must be completed correctly in order to preserve your claim and because it may vary from state to state, it is important to obtain competent legal counsel before beginning.

Title VII first requires that the charge be filed with a state agency if the violation occurs within a state that has set up an agency for handling discrimination claims. If your state does not have its own human rights commission or similar agency, you should file directly with the EEOC. Practically speaking, this means contacting the state agency or EEOC in your state by telephone and informing them that you wish to file a complaint. They will then instruct you on how and where to fill out the necessary paper work. In states that have an agency for handling these claims, filing with the state agency must be followed by timely filing the charge with the EEOC. Some state agencies will do this for you.

Usually the complaint must be filed within 180 days of the discriminatory act. The time period is measured from the date that the discriminatory act occurred. Upon the filing of the charge there is a 180 day mandatory waiting period, during which time the EEOC is given the opportunity to mediate and resolve the complaint. The private litigant then has 90 days in which to file suit. This limitation period runs not from the discriminatory act, but from the date the private party receives notice from the EEOC or state agency that conciliation was completed, or the date the party receives a right to sue letter.

Chapter Three

Government Employees

Government employees are protected by both Title VII and the United States Constitution against religious discrimination. Public employees do not forfeit their First Amendment rights upon entering the public workplace.[140] Therefore, the religious freedom of government employees has the additional protection of the Free Exercise and Free Speech Clauses of the First Amendment to the United States Constitution. This chapter explains how government employees are protected by the First Amendment above and beyond the protection they have from Title VII.

Q As a government employee, is all my religious speech at work protected by the First Amendment?

A A public employee receives greater speech protection when speaking "as a citizen upon matters of public concern" than he does when commenting on employment matters of personal or internal interest.[141] When evaluating these cases, the Supreme Court has traditionally utilized a test which balances the importance of the employee's speech on a matter of public concern against the government's need to run an efficient workplace.[142] Religious speech will always be a matter of public concern.

For example, in *Tucker v. State of California Dept. of Educ.*,[143] a federal Court of Appeals found religious speech to be a matter of public concern, and protected the religious liberties of a state education department employee who believed that he was commanded to "give

92

credit to God for the work he perform[ed]." He engaged in religious discussions, and kept religious material around his work area. Tucker prevailed when the court weighed the state's asserted interests of efficiency, protecting the liberty interests of other employees, and avoiding Establishment Clause issues against the weight of a "broad ban on group speech." The court rejected the employer's contention that the religious speech reduced efficiency since other types of non-work related speech were permitted. The court also rejected the argument that the employee's speech violated the Establishment Clause because there was no way it could have been attributed to the state.

Therefore, religious speech of government employees is protected so long as it does not significantly reduce efficiency in the workplace, and so long as it will not be attributed to the government employer.

Q As a government employee, can I keep religious items in my personal work area?

A The First Amendment also protects the right of public employees to keep items with religious messages on them at their desk. In a case where an employee had a Bible and plaques containing the serenity prayer, the Lord's Prayer, and one that said, "God be in my life and in my commitment" in his office, the government employer violated the First Amendment when it demanded that these items be removed because they might be considered "offensive to employees." [144] The fact that other employees may find these items offensive is irrelevant when considered in light of First Amendment freedoms. [145]

Q As a government employee, can I advertise events at my church on the bulletin board at work?

A If a government employer allows employees to post non-work related material around the office, they cannot prohibit the posting of religious material. "[I]t is not reasonable to allow employees to post materials around the office on all sorts of subjects, and forbid only the posting of religious information and materials."[146] Religious speech is given the same expansive protections offered to secular speech inviting "employees to motorcycle rallies, swap meets, x-rated movies, beer busts, or burlesque shows." Allowing this speech while prohibiting advertising for religious events "is unreasonable not only because it bans a vast amount of material without legitimate justification but also because its sole target is religious speech." [147]

Q Doesn't religious speech by government employees violate the "Separation Between Church and State?"

A The oft cited phrase "separation between church and state" is found nowhere in the Constitution. This phrase has been misused by many in this country to mislead people and trick them into believing that the government can have absolutely nothing to do with religion. The truth is the Constitution only prohibits the establishment of religion through the Establishment Clause of the First Amendment.

The Establishment Clause of the First Amendment does not provide the government with any justification for prohibiting religious expression in the workplace [148] As the United States Supreme Court said in this regard: "The Establishment Clause does not license government to treat religion and those who teach or practice it, simply by virtue of their status as such, as subversive of American ideals and therefore subject to unique disabilities."[149]

"We emphasize, too, that fear alone, even fear of discrimination or other illegal activity, is not enough to justify such a mobilization of governmental force against [an employee].... A phobia of religion, for instance, no matter how real subjectively, will not do. As Justice Brandeis has said,....' Men feared witches and burnt women."[150]

In August of 1997, President Clinton took the remarkable step of issuing guidelines confirming that federal workers can express their faith on the job. These guidelines direct federal agencies to "permit personal religious expression by federal employees to the greatest extent possible...."[151]

In sum, governmental employers may restrict religious activity in the workplace only if it prohibits the government from running an efficient workplace, or there is clear evidence that it is intimidating or harassing to co-workers. Speculative fears of offense or employee discontent do not provide the government with an excuse for discriminating against religious employees who express their faith through words, actions, or symbols.

Religious Activities By Employers Under Title VII

Chapter Four

Employer Religious Beliefs

Many employers have sincerely held religious beliefs which they want their businesses to reflect. But federal and state laws prohibiting religious discrimination in employment have discouraged many business owners from communicating their religious convictions at work. The good news is that, just like employees, business owners do not have to check their religion at the door when they come to work. The following information provides some guidance for religious employers who want their business to reflect their faith.

Q Do employers unlawfully discriminate if they base business objectives and goals upon Biblical principles?

A No. An employer does not discriminate on the basis of religion by affirming the faith of its owners in business objectives. [152] "Title VII does not, and could not, require individual employers to abandon their religion." [153] Employers must be careful, however, not to give prospective or current employees the perception that employment or advancement with the company depends on acquiescence in the religious beliefs of the employer. This can be accomplished in a number of ways. For instance, applications for employment should state that applicants are considered for all positions without regard to religion. This statement should also be included in any orientation materials, employee handbooks, and employee evaluation forms. Of course, employers must also be sure that this statement is accurate by not discriminating on the basis of religion.

Q As the owner of the business, can I witness to my employees?

A An employer can talk about his religious beliefs with employees as long as employees know that continued employment or advancement within the company is not conditioned upon acquiescence in the employer's religious beliefs. For instance, one court has held that an employer did not discriminate against an employee by sharing the gospel with him and inviting him to church.[154] Employers must be careful, however, not to persist in witnessing if the employee objects. Such unwanted proselytizing could be deemed religious harassment. Employers cannot impose their religious beliefs on their employees.[155]

Q Am I permitted to give my employees religious literature?

A As with spoken religious speech, employers can share their religious beliefs with their employees in print form such as pamphlets, books, and newsletters.[156] Employers must be careful, however, not to give employees the impression that they have to agree with the employer's religious beliefs in order to keep their job or get a promotion. For instance, in one case a Jewish employee was wrongfully terminated for complaining about the printing of Bible verses on his paychecks and the religious content of a company newsletter.[157] If an employer shares religious convictions with employees, and the employee disagrees or protests, no adverse action can be taken against the employee.

Furthermore, employers should be ready to accommodate any employee's objections to the religious speech contained in publications distributed to employees. Sufficient accommodation may be to provide the objecting employee with a publication that does not contain the religious content. In order to counter any impression given by publications that job security and advancement are contingent upon faith, it is also recommended that publications with religious material state that the employer does not discriminate on the basis of religion for purposes of continued employment, employee benefits, or promotion.

Q Can an employer hold regular prayer meetings or chaplain services for employees?

A Employers can hold regular devotional meetings for employees so long as attendance is not required. [158] Moreover, active participation of management in these meetings does not make them discriminatory. [159] To ensure that employees understand that devotional meetings are voluntary, notice of the meetings should state that they are not mandatory and it is wise to hold these meetings before the work day begins, during breaks, or after work.

Q Can I require my employees to attend training based on Biblical principles?

A Employers can use training programs that are based on the Bible. For instance, requiring an employee to attend a management seminar put on by the Institute of Basic Life Principles which used scriptural passages to support the lessons it sought to promote did not violate a Massachusetts civil rights law. [160] Employees cannot, however, be required to undergo religious training, participate in religious services, or engage in behavior that would violate their sincerely held religious beliefs.

Appendix One
Title VII Overview

A. Threshold Requirements For Title VII Coverage

Title VII applies to most large private employers as well as to governmental employers. With regard to employers, Title VII states:

(a) Employer practices.

It shall be an unlawful employment practice for an employer:

(1) to fail or refuse to hire or to discharge any individual, or otherwise to discriminate against any individual with respect to his compensation, terms, conditions, or privileges of employment, because of such individual's race, color, religion, sex, or national origin; or

(2) to limit, segregate, or classify his employees or applicants for employment in any way which would deprive or tend to deprive any individual of employment opportunities or otherwise adversely affect his status as an employee, because of such individual's race, color, religion, sex or national

origin. 42 U.S.C. § 2000e-2. Title VII defines "employer" as "a person engaged in an industry affecting commerce who has fifteen or more employees for each working day in each of twenty or more calendar weeks in the current or preceding calendar year, and any agent of such a person...." 42 U.S.C. § 2000e(b). Title VII therefore covers an employer who has fifteen or more employees on his payroll for at least twenty weeks during a given year. Once coverage is established in a given year, Title VII coverage will extend through the following year, even if the number of employees falls below the minimum.

As to what is an "employee," the statute is not limited to traditional definitions of employees. "Employee" includes all who "are susceptible to the kind of unlawful practices that Title VII was intended to remedy." [161] Thus, Title VII may apply even if the employee is an independent contractor.

The statute also applies to state and local governments through 42 U.S.C. § 2000e(a), and to the federal government via 42 U.S.C. § 2000e-16. In fact, Title VII is the exclusive judicial remedy offering injunctive relief for discrimination in federal employment. [162] Title VII does not apply to religious organizations. 42 U.S.C. § 2000e-1. 42 U.S.C. § 2000e-2(b) - (d) brings employment agencies, labor organizations, and training programs under the umbrella of Title VII.

B. Title VII Procedures: Private Defendants

1. Deferral to State Agencies

The majority of jurisdictions have "deferral agencies," typically denoted as a "state equal employment opportunity agency" or "human rights commission." These are state or local agencies authorized to seek or grant relief from the discriminatory practice or to institute criminal proceedings. 42 U.S.C. § 2000e-5(c). Charges must be filed with both the state or local agency as well as with the EEOC. The EEOC is required by statute to allow a deferral agency not less than 60 days after the charge is filed to dispose of the charge. 42 U.S.C. § 2000e-5(d). The majority of states require a charge to be filed with their deferral agency within 180 days following the act of discrimination.

In deferral jurisdictions EEOC has no jurisdiction unless a timely charge is first filed with the deferral agency. Although EEOC may initially accept a charge and file with the state agency on its own initiative, this should not be relied upon. The aggrieved party should file a timely charge directly with the deferral agency to ensure meeting this prerequisite to filing suit. A local agency may waive its 60-day deferral period through a worksharing agreement with the EEOC, thus "terminating" the agency's proceedings so that the EEOC may deem a charge filed and begin processing it.

2. Filing with the EEOC

In states without a deferral agency, charges of specific discriminatory acts must be filed with the EEOC within 180 days after the discriminatory act occurred. [163] This and other time periods specified by Title VII may be tolled when equity demands modification. [164] Where there is a state deferral agency, the time period for filing with the EEOC is extended to 300 days, or within 30 days after receiving notice that

101

the state has terminated the proceedings under state or local law, whichever is earlier.[165] The EEOC may, if it receives the charge first, file the state charge on its own initiative and then automatically re-file the charge with itself after the 60-day deferral period expires. [166] The surest course of action, however, is to directly file the EEOC charge once the state deferral period expires or the state terminates its investigation, whichever comes first.[167]

Once the charge is timely filed, EEOC has 180 days of exclusive jurisdiction over the charge. Because the state deferral period is mandatory, the combined effect is that a plaintiff must first await the results of state efforts for 60 days, then ensure that an EEOC charge is filed, and then await the results of EEOC conciliation efforts for 180 days. There is no statute of limitation on the EEOC's investigation and conciliation efforts.

3. Civil Actions by the EEOC or by the Aggrieved Party

The EEOC may bring a civil action if it fails to secure a conciliation agreement within 30 days of either the charge being filed with EEOC or the 60 day state deferral period expiring.[168] If the EEOC dismisses a charge filed with it, or if the EEOC fails to file a civil action within 180 days of exclusive jurisdiction, then the EEOC must so notify the person aggrieved.[169] Alternatively, when EEOC conciliation efforts extend past the 180 days of exclusive EEOC jurisdiction, the aggrieved person need not await the outcome of conciliation but may instead request a "notice-of-right-to-sue." In either circumstance, the aggrieved person may then bring a civil action on his own behalf within 90 days of receipt of such notice.[170] Should the aggrieved person allow the EEOC to continue its conciliation efforts past the exclusive jurisdiction period, he may file suit if the final EEOC resolution is adverse to him, even if the conciliation takes years to complete.

In the case where the aggrieved person is a state or local government employee and the Commission fails to secure a conciliation agreement, it must refer the case to the Attorney General. The person aggrieved has a right to intervene in a civil action brought by the Commission or the Attorney General.[171] The charging party may bring suit on his behalf subject to the same limitations above. After suit is filed, the EEOC is precluded from filing an independent action.

In summary, Title VII first requires that the charge be filed with the deferral agency if within a deferral jurisdiction, or directly with the EEOC if not. In deferral jurisdictions, filing with the deferral agency must be followed by timely filing the charge with the EEOC. The time periods are measured from the date that the discriminatory act occurred. Upon filing of the charge there is a 180 day mandatory waiting period, during which time the EEOC is given the opportunity to mediate and resolve the complaint. The private litigant then has 90 days in which to file suit. This limitation period runs not from the discriminatory act, but from the date the private party receives notice from the EEOC because either conciliation was completed or the party requested a right to sue letter.

C. Title VII Procedures: Federal Defendants

Title VII requires

federal defendants to use significantly different procedures. Within the federal government the employing agency is the primary administrator for Title VII. Claims are filed with Equal Employment Opportunity Counselors within the offending agency, not with the EEOC. Before a formal claim is filed, the aggrieved person must file a "pre-complaint" notice with a counselor within 45 days of the discriminatory act.[172] The counselor must attempt to resolve the dispute within 30 days.[173] At the end of the dispute resolution period, a final interview is conducted with the aggrieved party. If the matter has not been resolved, written notice is given to the aggrieved party. Formal charges may then be filed with "appropriate agency officials" within 15 days of receipt of that notice.[174] The agency then has 180 days from filing to resolve the complaint; at the end of this period, the complainant may either request a hearing before an administrative law judge or accept a final agency disposition without further hearings.[175]

The aggrieved party need not wait for the administrative procedures to run their full course. A civil action in federal district court may be commenced when 180 days have elapsed since the filing of the formal complaint.[176] If the agency has made a determination on the formal charge, the aggrieved party may file suit within 90 days of receipt of the "decision letter."[177]

Alternatively, the agency's final decision or dismissal of the complaint may be appealed to the EEOC within 30 days of receiving the decision letter.[178] As of 1997, there is no set time period limiting the length of appellate review by the

EEOC.[179] Once EEOC issues a final decision on the appeal, the aggrieved party has 90 days from receipt of the final decision to file a civil action.[180]

Section Six

MAKING A DIFFERENCE: Changing Local Laws

Chapter One

A Strategy Session

Here I want to explore ways to protect First Amendment freedoms without resorting to the courtroom. Issues brought before public local government meetings are often best dealt with by an attorney. Addressing school board or city council meetings may require an in depth knowledge of the law and how it works. It may even require the same preparation as an attorney puts into developing a court case. The American Center for Law and Justice has vast experience handling school boards and city councils. We have sent attorneys to these meetings around the country. By using the strategies that follow, we have been able to resolve serious problems successfully without ever going to court.

Local school boards and city councils are appropriate bodies for hearing concerns on a wide variety of issues. For example, school boards consider issues involving school curricula, school facility access (for example, whether they must allow religious groups to use school facilities after school hours), and students' rights on campus. Students' rights on campus include the right to distribute literature, the right to initiate and participate in a Bible club during the school day, the right to pray with friends during the day or before school starts, the right to wear Christian T-shirts, the right to bring a Bible to school and read it during free time, the right to pray at graduation ceremonies, the right to make a speech giving God glory during graduation, and the right to hold a baccalaureate service during the graduation season. Each of these issues are appropriate for going before the school board and voicing an opinion on what the school board must do to secure students' constitutional rights.

City councils and other local government bodies also have a wide range of issues with which they are concerned. Some of these are: evangelism in public places, such as city streets, sidewalks and local public parks; concerts in public parks; rallies or Christian crusades in public facilities;

such as the city auditorium or civic center; the right to distribute literature in public places, such as streets, sidewalks and public parks; pornography ordinances; and zoning ordinances involving churches and parade ordinances for marches on public streets. You can go before your city council and express your opinion on what the city council must do to secure local citizens' or churches' constitutional rights in these areas and others.

While I recommend that attorneys make the presentations to local school boards and city councils, I wrote this section to educate people who have no legal training so they could walk into a board or council meeting and comfortably present an issue and request the board or council to resolve the problem.

If you happen to be an attorney, it is important for you to approach your presentation before a school board or city council the same way you would approach a presentation before a court. These civic bodies are filled with professionals who appreciate a well thought-out, thorough, concise presentation. You cannot be too prepared.

If you are not an attorney, the principles found in this section will still help you prepare for a school board or city council meeting.

The law is clear: First Amendment freedoms must be protected. However, it is important how the law concerning these freedoms is presented to local school boards and city councils. The responsibility of representing First Amendment issues before school boards and city councils requires a spokesperson who is able to utilize a wide range of skills, including abilities in legal research, negotiation, communications and public relations. This type of representation demands not only proficiency in a variety of procedures, but also a mindfulness of sensitive local issues since the community is so directly involved.

Preliminary evaluation is essential to a successful presentation. You must closely examine the facts. Then these facts must be applied to the legal precedents in your area and the Supreme Court. If you fail to properly evaluate your case, the entire presentation could be off-base and ineffective. Once you evaluate these components, you must weigh them in the context of the theory and nature of the result desired. For example, your presentation might be before a local city council who has forbidden the distribution of literature on city streets because of the littering problem. Rather than spend the entire meeting on the right to distribute literature under the First Amendment, you could simply point out that the Supreme Court has held that littering ordinances are invalid when they are used to stop otherwise protected free speech.

The sense of community goodwill you bring to your case and presentation cannot be over emphasized. Local leaders, including school officials, school board members, city council members, attorneys, and the media need to understand that you support them while attempting to resolve the issues in question. It is in the best interest of all parties if you can diffuse potentially explosive situations early in the process.

In addition to these matters, it is very important that you factor in the very nature of the action itself. A contention over the free speech attributes of the distribution of literature might not awaken the general population. But the recent issues revolving around graduation prayer could stimulate the entire community, including both school board officials and their attorneys on the local and state level. A case involving equal access to public facilities can serve as a rallying point for the Christian community in garnering local support. In all these situations, the spokesperson plays a key role in assuring that all parties maintain the proper perspective and that you understand the implications involved.

At the heart of any dispute or discussion with school boards or city councils is the particular strategy chosen to resolve the problem successfully. Even though attorneys are trained to evaluate and litigate, there are times when the concern about litigation from a social and/or biblical perspective closes the door to litigation, thereby making an out-of-court settlement the only way to resolve the dispute. Out-of-court settlements can help to establish good rapport with local officials, which can lead to alliance building that can be quite useful in future situations.

With the emergence of new rulings on these and related issues, it is absolutely necessary that a presenter engage in accurate research and interpretation of case law. While this may be overlooked, failure to accurately identify legal issues relevant to the case and then apply the necessary legal authority can easily result in disaster.

On the other hand, attention to the details of defending clients before school boards and city councils can yield more than a successful resolution — it can foster long-term working relationships within the community which can foster a more accepting environment for the exercise of First Amendment freedoms.

Chapter Two

Practical Tips For Making Your Case

Q Why should I consider the strategy of working through the local government group that decides who is allowed access to property under its control?
A Our job as Christians is to share the Gospel and confront contemporary issues from a biblical perspective. At the American Center, our goal is to keep open all channels of communication so our message can be heard in the public arena, not just in our homes and churches. When a school board or city council has wrongfully denied some-

one the right to proclaim the Gospel, a channel for preaching and evangelism is lost. We want to reopen that channel as quickly as possible.

Q Why are local boards and councils a good place to change policies in the community?

A Local government bodies are the first line of decision-making. Local schools are primarily run by local school boards, not courts or state school boards. Student free speech is most often blocked by *local* regulations, not state regulations. City parks and sidewalks are most often shut down by *local* city commissions rather than by state regulations.

Local board and council members are usually elected. Elected officials are very sensitive to the fact that an unhappy public is not the best way to get reelected. Most public officials desire to be reelected. When the coverage they receive is negative, board or council members want to change that image. That means they are more likely to get on the side of parents and other citizens who can rally support for a local board meeting. Why? Because these same people can also rally votes during election time. Politicians need vote getters, not just voters, so their ears perk up when support looms large for a cause they may have not championed in the past.

Additionally, boards and councils make policies that affect the local communities they govern. While Washington, D.C., is far away, the local courthouse or boardroom is just around the corner. The local board's influence is more readily felt by the community, hence it is a good place to start when changing local policies.

Moreover, by working through a local board, two potential problems are avoided. First, there is the problem of time. Boards often make a wrong decision based on misinformation. They wrongly believe they have the authority to discriminate against Christian speech because of the so-called "separation of church and state." If the local board can be educated, the problem can be resolved within days rather than the months, even years, it could take to work the matter through the courts. Therefore, to save valuable time and energy, not to mention financial resources, the best strategy is often to go straight to the local board to resolve the problem.

The other problem is community relations. By educating the board, a local Christian church or group can resolve the misunderstanding that has created the problem without offending the community in the process. The public does not have an accurate concept of the legal process and, therefore, they often view all litigation as hostile. So while a court battle may be won, the community relations war will have been lost. This does not mean a matter should never be litigated. If negotiations fail or education proves impossible, the option of a legal remedy in the courtroom still exists. Nevertheless, whenever possible, resolving the case through the local boards is the better approach. In fact, especially in tight economic times, what local government group would sacrifice the opportunity to save taxpayers' money while upholding the Constitution just to win a court case? Local officials do not relish court battles any more than anyone else. If you can help them avoid one, they may rise up and call you blessed.

Q How do I get on the agenda?

A Usually agendas are set one to several months in advance. Therefore, preplanning must begin early enough to allow the political machinery time to function. If a person approaches the board on a Monday just before a Tuesday board meeting, the chairman of the board may or may not allow her to appear on the agenda and address the board. If that same person had requested at a much earlier time that she be placed on the agenda it would have been no problem.

If you are from out of town, you might want to have the client or some other local person get your name on the agenda. But be sure to follow up on your request. Some-

times the local person may be convinced that the board or council is putting you on the agenda, but he has not checked to ensure that this is the case. Never assume you are on the agenda. A quick phone call will determine if the proper steps have been followed and you are on board to speak. Our attorneys always place a follow-up phone call to ensure they are on the board or council meeting agenda. This helps avoid unnecessary expense and undue embarrassment.

Q How do I build community support before the board meeting?

A Work with your local churches. When a local church sees the need for involvement, they will sound the cry for help. A pastor is in a good position to explain the need to his congregation once he knows what the need is.

Many communities have groups in place that are involved in local political issues. These groups have the contacts needed to alert the community. They usually have close relationships with at least one or two local churches. Therefore, local community action groups can be very helpful in building community support that will help affect changes in your area.

Q How do I lay the proper groundwork for the maximum effect in the community?

A In addition to appealing to local churches, there are several other ways to lay the proper groundwork for the maximum effect in your community. Most communities have para-church organizations that are willing to help heighten community awareness. Because these organizations work with different churches rather than within any one church, they are better able to spread the word to more members of the community. One of the roles of a para-church ministry is to develop contacts in and around the community. These contacts can be helpful in a campaign designed to stimulate community awareness.

Local and national civic groups are another way of involving the local community. These groups constantly look for worthy projects to sponsor. Like a para-church ministry, civic groups draw people from a variety of lifestyles which serves to heighten community awareness.

It is important to have the people who are affected by the board or council decision at the meeting. If the school board is voting on an issue that affects students in the community, it is helpful to have students present. Often we request that students be allowed to address the school board as well as our attorney. This assures that the school board realizes that the vote they are about to take affects real lives. We ask parents to come as well. By their presence, parents send a two-fold message: they are concerned about the decisions that affect their children; they are voters and this meeting might well determine how they vote. This approach is not manipulation; it is the American political process at work.

The same approach should be taken with a city council. Whoever will be affected by the council vote should be present at the meeting. We often request time for them to address the council members for the same reason we ask students to address a school board.

Every person present at a board or council meeting represents a percentage of the community. By attending a meeting we let elected officials know we are watching how they vote. This monitoring devise was built into our system by our founding fathers. It reminds our political leaders that if they do not do what the people want, the people have the right to elect someone else. Our political system works best when people are involved in the process. Apathy destroys the system; participation improves it.

Q Should I involve the press?

A We seldom speak to the press before we go into court. Board and council presentations, however, present a different situation. Boards and councils are political bodies and therefore, by definition, more subject to community pressure than a court — and rightly so.

The press can make a poorly-attended board or council meeting a hot item in the community. Suddenly, the school board or city council is looking at several hundred parents or citizens who expect to get a satisfactory answer from them at that meeting. Each of these parents or citizens translates into a person who is concerned enough to take the time to attend a meeting. If they are that concerned, they are most likely concerned enough to vote and influence others to vote too. The press can alert the community to a need of which they may have been unaware. Many Christians view the press as an enemy, and never stop to realize that the local press often merely presents local community happenings. Christians should learn to alert the press about particular events. We should be willing to use the press to alert the community of the decisions of local political leaders, such as school boards or city council members. Publicity often brings accountability to local political bodies.

Q When I am appearing before a board, should I use a written presentation or speak entirely extemporaneously?
A It is important to be prepared when speaking to boards or councils. The benefit of preparing a written statement is that it forces focus. When speaking at meetings such as a school board or a city council, time is usually very limited. Members of those bodies work full-time jobs and

115

appreciate brevity. Lengthy addresses tend to distract from your role as counselor and concerned citizen. They can also create confusion rather than resolve it, since longer talks tend to ramble.

When you come before the board with a prepared text, the facts will be clear in your head, the law will be on the tip of your tongue, and you will speak with greater eloquence and clarity. That will cause you to stand out before the board and give greater credibility to your comments.

This does not mean, though, that you should be inflexible. After all, situations can change and cause your speech to be outdated. For example, one of our attorneys was speaking to a park commission in Boston, Massachusetts. He had prepared a statement for the commissioners in antici-pation of their meeting. All prior indications led to the conclusion that the commission would not attempt to censor the religious speech of a local pastor in their park, so our attorney's prepared speech was very concilia-tory. As the meeting began, however, it became obvious that even though the board would agree to allow the pastor to speak in the park, board members were unhappy that they were being "forced' to allow the speech to occur uncensored. Hence, our attorney's prepared talk had to be adapted to fit the unexpected situation. If he had delivered it as originally written, it would have missed the point. Was it therefore a wasted effort? Not at all. The prepared speech allowed our attorney to be knowledgeable enough about the situation to effectively and forcefully adapt his presentation to fit the need of the moment.

Q How do I make my oral presentation to the board?

A Any time you address a board or council you must remember to be animated and forceful without being obnoxious or arrogant. Let the tone of your presentation reflect the mood of the board or council. If the board is working to resolve the problem, you should be forceful yet friendly. If the board is dragging their feet, you should be forceful and insistent. If the board is refusing to protect your or your client's First Amendment freedoms, you should be forceful and aggressive. Remember, boards and councils are political bodies; they will respond to community pressure. A well-argued, powerful presentation may well influence them to protect First Amendment freedoms.

Also, boards and councils see a host of presentations during the course of a year. Their time is limited and they have many things on their minds when you are there. So grab their attention by being knowledgeable. Do not force them to guess what you want — tell them straight out. And in the process, lay out the facts and the law in the same way you would to a court, while being conscious of the fact that your audience is not likely composed of lawyers. Remember, board or council members are not as aware of the situation as you are, especially the situation as viewed through your client's eyes. So make sure your presentation fosters clarity and understanding at every turn. Board and council members are not mind readers; they must be told what is expected of them by you and the Constitution and why.

Q Once I have spoken to the board or council, is my job through?

A No. Follow-up is probably the most important job you have when you are working with a local school board or city council. These boards and councils are administrative bodies, and often an idea gets lost or confused on the way from the meeting to the application of the idea. The process of reaching a decision is filled with give and take. Confusion often develops during the course of a meeting as to what the board or council members are merely discussing, and what the board or council has actually decided. After a decision has been reached, the decision will often be written out for clarity's sake. While the board or council may sincerely intend for the idea to be implemented the way it was discussed during the meeting, the clerk, or whoever types up the decision, may not convey what the board intended. Additionally, whenever communication takes place, there is always the potential for misunderstanding. Because people approach conversations and negotiations from different vantage points, they may leave a discussion thinking that the other side is happy - only to discover that when the terms of the agreement are finally reduced to writing, the written statement does not represent what each side thought they had agreed to. Therefore, you should always follow up a presentation or negotiation.

Follow-up is simple. A phone call or letter is usually adequate to confirm that everything is moving ahead properly. At the American Center, we always follow up our presentations with a letter. Usually we request a copy of any decisions or rules that came from the meeting. It also allows us to look over what the board or council agreed to and evaluate the new guidelines in light of what is legal and what best serves the interests of our client.

Q What result has the American Center seen from addressing the problem at the board and council meeting level rather than in the courtroom?

A The results have been extremely favorable. When we attend board and council meetings, we are there on behalf of members of the local community. We are there with a full knowledge of the constitutional principles involved. We are there to help resolve the problem. We do not approach the board or council with haughtiness, yet we are prepared to stand up for the rights of Christians. To this point, we have never been to a board or council meeting where we were unable to work out a solution that was acceptable to the people we represented.

Our government was originally designed to work according to the desires of the people. Government must be responsive to the voice of the governed if it is to be effective. When you attend a board or council meeting and speak up, your voice is heard. Local government bodies are very responsive to the voice of the governed, even though that is less often the case with national government bodies. Local board and council members realize they have to look local citizens in the eye after they make their decisions. Your presence and voice at a local board or council meeting can make a difference, but you must be prepared.

APPENDIX I

STUDENTS' RIGHTS LEGAL BRIEFING

The Federal Constitution

Students are vested with two distinct sets of rights in the public school setting. First, all students retain their constitutionally protected right to freedom of speech and expression. Second, the federal Equal Access Act guarantees high school students the right to have Bible clubs on campus.

The Supreme Court has addressed the right of students to express their opinions on their public school campuses. Specifically, the Court has held that students and teachers do not "shed their constitutional rights . . . at the schoolhouse gate." [181] This principle means that students rightfully on a public school campus have First Amendment rights that cannot be denied without reason. It is important to note that the 8th Circuit in *Mergens* held that students have a First Amendment right and an Equal Access Act right to hold a student-initiated Bible club meeting on campus. [182] Thus, even in the event that a school has not allowed any noncurriculum clubs to meet, the Tinker rule would still require that students be allowed to associate with other students in Bible clubs. School officials must be very careful about abridging the rights of students who are rightfully on campus.

Material or Substantial Disruption: The Heart of Tinker

Under the *Tinker* decision, a principal cannot prohibit student speech simply because he believes there will be a disruption of the educational process. In fact, he can only restrict student speech if it will "materially or substantially disrupt school discipline." [183] Students have the right to discuss religious beliefs, and even share religious materials, with their peers between classes, at break, at lunch, and before and after school. As the Court declared:

> *It can hardly be argued that either students or teachers shed their constitutional rights to freedom of speech or expression at the schoolhouse gate. This has been the unmistakable holding of this Court for almost 50 years.* [184]

In the nearly 25 years since *Tinker*, the Supreme Court has continued this holding. It has now been the Court's holding for almost 75 years.

Tinker's holding did not depend on a finding that the school was a public forum. The Court emphasized, instead, that "[w]hen [a student] is in the cafeteria, or on the playing field, or on the campus during the authorized hours, he may express his opinions...." [185] Therefore, whether or not a school campus constitutes a public forum for nonstudents, it is clear that the students who are required to attend have the protection of First Amendment Free Speech guarantees.

Fundamental Rights of Students

Our educational system requires students to attend schools. This coercion gives students the legal right to be on campus. As Justice Fortas noted:

> *In our system, state-operated schools may not be enclaves of totalitarianism. School officials do not possess absolute*

121

authority over their students. Students in school as well as out of school are "persons" under our Constitution. They are possessed of fundamental rights which the State must respect, just as they themselves must respect their obligations to the State. In our system, students may not be regarded as closed-circuit recipients of only that which the State chooses to communicate. They may not be confined to the expression of those sentiments that are officially approved. In the absence of a specific showing of constitutionally valid reasons to regulate their speech, students are entitled to freedom of expression of their views. As Judge Gewin speaking for the

Fifth Circuit, said, school officials cannot suppress "expressions of feelings with which they do not wish to contend." [186]

Student Rights On Campus After *Tinker*

After *Tinker*, the law regarding the First Amendment rights of students is well-established. Student speech cannot be restricted because of the content of that speech. School administrators can only prohibit protected speech by students when it "materially and substantially interfere[s] with the requirements of appropriate discipline in the operation of the school." [187]

It is well settled that religious speech is protected by the First Amendment of the Constitution, even when that speech is taking place on the public school campus.[188] In fact, the right to persuade, advocate or evangelize a religious viewpoint, implicates the very reason the First Amendment was adopted. As the Supreme Court held in *Thomas v. Collins*:

> [T]he protection [the Framers] saw was not solely for persons in intellectual pursuits. It extends to more than abstract discussion unrelated to action. The First Amendment is a charter for government, not for an institution of learning. **Free trade in ideas** means free trade and the opportunity to persuade, not merely to describe facts.[189]

The nature of public schools does not justify the forfeiture of Constitutional rights. In fact, the public nature of such schools enhances the Constitutional rights of students. The school is the best place to teach students how the laws of the land apply.

The Equal Access Act

The Supreme Court held, in *Widmar v. Vincent*, that when colleges allowed student groups to use their facilities they could not discriminate against student religious groups.[190] In other words, Christian students have to be allowed to use a meeting room on campus with the same restrictions applied to any other student group. The Establishment Clause of the First Amendment is not violated when a government entity, such as a public university, treats all groups the same, without attempting to censor religious speech. The *Mergens* Court quoted from *Widmar* extensively as they explained why secondary students have the right to have religious clubs on their campus.

Congress enacted the Equal Access Act to cure pervasive antireligious bigotry exhibited by public secondary school officials in the aftermath of the Supreme Court's school prayer cases. Three factors determine whether the Equal Access Act compels official recognition of a Bible club by school officials: 1) does the school receive federal funds; 2) is the school a public secondary school; and 3) does the school allow any noncurriculum clubs to meet on campus?

When these factors are satisfied, federal law compels school officials to provide equal access to students who want to organize and conduct Bible clubs and student prayer groups.

In *Garnett v. Renton School Dist. No. 403*, a Federal Court of Appeals ruled that the Equal Access Act must be complied with even in the face of a state constitutional provision to the contrary. [191]

Westside Community Schools v. Mergens

The United States Supreme Court upheld the constitutionality of the Equal Access Act in *Westside Community Schools v. Mergens* (*Mergens*).[192] According to the *Mergens* Court, the above-mentioned factors should be employed in a standard three-prong analysis, as follows:

1. Federal Funding. Does the school receive any federal funds at all? This question is answered, simply, yes or no. If the answer is no, the Equal Access Act does not apply. If the answer is yes, it is necessary to examine the next prong of the *Mergens*-Equal Access Act test.

2. Secondary Schools. Is the school in question a secondary school as defined by state law? This information should be available from the local State Board of Education. If the school in question is classified as a secondary school, it is then necessary to examine the third prong of the *Mergens*-Equal Access Act test. While it varies from state to state, most states classify a secondary school as grades nine through twelve.

3. Noncurriculum Clubs on Campus.

Does the school allow noncurriculum clubs to meet on campus? Here the *Mergens* Court was very specific. Schools cannot misrepresent the nature of clubs that are permitted to meet. The Court explicitly examined the intent of Congress concerning noncurriculum-related clubs:

> *[W]e think that the term 'noncurriculum related student group' is best interpreted broadly to mean any student group that does not directly relate to the body of courses offered by the school. In our view, a student group directly relates to a school's curriculum if the subject matter of the group is actually taught, or will soon be taught, in a regularly offered course; if the subject matter of the group concerns the body of courses as a whole; if participation in the group is required for a particular course; or if participation in the group results in academic credit. . . . This . . . definition . . . is consistent with Congress' intent to provide a low threshold for triggering the [Equal Access] Act's requirements.* [193]

Thus, the nature of the clubs currently meeting at the school is key. Service clubs, for example, such as the Key Club, the Lions Club, Zonta and Interact are not considered curriculum-related.

Additionally, clubs such as the Chess Club do

125

not relate to the curriculum under normal circumstances. For example, only when a school teaches chess as an academic subject, for which students received a grade, would a Chess Club be considered related to the curriculum. The school district's argument, in *Mergens*, that chess was curriculum related because it enhanced logical thinking and the performance of mathematical calculations, was rejected by the Supreme Court.

In *Mergens*, Justice O'Connor noted that "if a state refused to let religious groups use the facilities open to others, then it would demonstrate not neutrality but hostility toward religion. The Establishment Clause does not license government to treat religion and those who teach or practice it, simply by virtue of their status as such, as subversive of American ideals and therefore subject to unique disabilities." [194] When a public high school official refuses to allow student-initiated Bible clubs treatment equal to that given other noncurriculum clubs meeting on campus, it treats those students as second-class citizens. This attitude is precisely the one which the Equal Access Act prohibits.

Bible Clubs Must Receive Official Recognition

Official recognition means that the Bible club must be treated the same as other clubs meeting on campus. "Official recognition allows student clubs to be part of the student activities program and carries with it access to the school newspaper, bulletin boards, the public address system, and the annual Club Fair." [195] Under that view, Bible clubs are allowed to advertise on campus. Types of advertisement could include, but are not limited to: flyers distributed among other students, posters displayed on the school walls, notices in the school newspaper and announcements included during the morning or afternoon announcements. It is important to note that the Bible club is not responsible to make sure the students know that the club is student-initiated. Rather, this is a responsibility of school officials.

Once the Equal Access Act is triggered, the school must provide a room for the Bible club. The school must also make its resources available to the Bible club in the same way that those resources are made available to other clubs. Additionally, the Bible club must be allowed to meet at any time other clubs are allowed to meet. If there is a club period, the Bible club must be allowed to meet during that period.

If other clubs are allowed to have school-wide assemblies to espouse their views, then the Bible club must be allowed the same privilege. Secondary school officials are not allowed to discriminate against a student group because of its message. Neither is a secondary school official allowed to censor the speech of the Bible Club by requiring it to delete references to Christianity from the club's constitution, announcements, or other materials.

Sponsors v. Custodians: Faculty/Staff

The only difference between a Bible club and any other club allowed to meet on the school campus is the use of faculty members as club sponsors. The Equal Access Act specifically allows for a faculty/staff custodian as compared to a normal club sponsor. This means that the faculty/staff custodian does not have control of the Bible club. He or she is only there to ensure that the Bible club does not violate school policies.

The Bible club must be student-initiated. This means that students must create and lead the club. It does not mean that they cannot have outside speakers. It only means that a non-student cannot lead the club. Community leaders and others can be invited to speak occasionally.

Literature Distribution

Students' First Amendment rights include the right to distribute Gospel tracts during non-instructional time, the right to wear shirts with overtly Christian messages and symbols, and the right to pray and discuss matters of religion with others. Further, schools may not prevent students from bringing their Bibles to school. In fact, school officials must allow students to read their Bibles during free time, even if that free time occurs during class. The standard that must be applied by the school is: Does the activity "materially or substantially disrupt school discipline?" Unless a student is participating in activities that are disruptive, the school must allow them to continue.

As a preliminary matter, it is a constitutional axiom that the distribution of free religious literature is a form of expression protected by the First Amendment. Religious and political speech are protected by the First Amendment. [196] Furthermore, "advocacy and persuasive speech are included within the First Amendment guarantee if the speech is otherwise protected."[197]

The United States

Supreme Court's consistent jurisprudence, for over 50 years, recognizes the free distribution of literature as a form of expression protected by the United States Constitution.[198] In *Lovell*, the United States Supreme Court put the case for constitutional protection of leaflets and pamphlets quite clearly:

> *The liberty of the press is not confined to newspapers and periodicals. It necessarily embraces pamphlets and leaflets. These indeed have been historic weapons in the defense of liberty, as the pamphlets of Thomas Paine and others in our history abundantly attest. The press in its historic connotation comprehends every sort of publication which affords a vehicle of information and opinion.*

> *What we have had recent occasion to say with respect to the vital importance of protecting this essential liberty from every sort of infringement need not be repeated.*[199]

Of course, the constitutional value of leaflets and pamphlets is not lessened by the fact that they address matters of religion. The materials at issue in *Lovell* were "a pamphlet and magazine in the nature of religious tracts. . . ."[200] Just five years after *Lovell*, in *Murdock v. Pennsylvania*, the United States Supreme Court said:

> *The hand distribution of religious tracts is an age – old form of missionary evangelism — as old as the history of printing presses. It has been a potent force in various religious movements down through the*

years. . . . It is more than preaching; it is more than distribution of religious literature. It is a combination of both. Its purpose is as evangelical as the revival meeting. This form of religious activity occupies the same high estate under the First Amendment as do worship in the churches and preaching from the pulpits.[201]

School officials may not lump a student's right to distribute free literature together with more disruptive forms of expression, such as solicitation. In a recent decision, a plurality of the Supreme Court noted the experience of thousands of "residents of metropolitan areas [who] know from daily experience [that] confrontation by a person asking for money disrupts passage and is more intrusive and intimidating than an encounter with a person giving out information."[202] In fact, distribution of literature is, inherently, even less disruptive than spoken expression. As the Supreme Court stated, "[o]ne need not ponder the contents of a leaflet or pamphlet in order mechanically to take it out of someone's hand, but one must listen, comprehend, decide and act in order to respond to a solicitation."[203]

The applicable standard - material and substantial disruption - is not met by an undifferentiated fear or apprehension of disruption. In other words, it is not enough for school officials to fear that allowing religious speech will offend some members of the community. As the Supreme Court said, "in our system, undifferentiated fear or apprehension of disturbance is not enough to overcome the right to freedom of expression."[204] Where a student wishes to peacefully distribute free literature on school grounds during non-instructional time, there simply is nothing which "might reasonably [lead] school authorities to forecast substantial disruption or material interference with school activities. . . ."[205] In fact, several courts have held that the distribution of religious literature by high school students is protected speech under the First Amendment and Fourteenth Amendment.[206] Note that in *Hemry* school officials ultimately conceded that students had the right to distribute the religious material on campus both inside and outside the school building.[207]

As the Supreme Court clearly held in *Tinker*:

In our system, state-operated schools may not be enclaves for totalitarianism. School officials do not possess absolute authority over their students. Students in school as well as out of school are persons under our Constitution. They are possessed of fundamental rights which the state must respect, just as they themselves must respect their obligations to the state. In our system, students may not be regarded as closed-circuit recipients of only that which the state chooses to communicate. They may not be confined to the expressions of those sentiments that are officially approved.[208]

While school officials may seek to distinguish *Tinker* as inapplicable by arguing that a public school is not a traditional public forum, such assertions are unavailing because "[the holding in

131

Tinker did not depend upon a finding that the school was a public forum." [209] As the *Tinker* Court noted, when a student "is in the cafeteria, or on the playing field, or on the campus during the authorized hours, he may express his opinions. . . ." [210]

Further, as the *Rivera* court noted, "whether or not a school campus is available as the public forum to others, it is clear that the students, who of course are required to be in school, have the protection of the First Amendment while they are lawfully in attendance." [211] The *Tinker* Court also recognized that "personal intercommunication among students" in high schools is an activity to which schools are dedicated. [212]

Certainly, it is necessary to acknowledge that school officials have "important, delicate and highly discretionary functions" to perform. [213]

These functions, however, must be performed "within the limits of the Bill of Rights." [214] "The vigilant protection of constitutional freedoms is nowhere more vital than in a community of American schools." [215]

School officials need not fear that distribution activities of students may be imputed to them, and that the Establishment Clause would thereby be violated. This very argument has been reviewed and rejected by the United States Supreme Court. In *Mergens*, the Supreme Court stated, as a general proposition, that the activities of student evangelists in a public school do not present any Establishment Clause problem:

Petitioner's principal contention is that the Act has the primary effect of advancing religion. Specifically, petitioners urge that, because the student religious meetings are held under school aegis, and because the state's compulsory attendance laws bring the students together (and thereby provide a readymade audience for student evangelists), an objective observer in the position of a secondary school student will perceive official school support for such religious meetings. . . We disagree. [216]

Of course, *Mergens* merely reflects the Establishment Clause's intended limitation — not on the rights of individual students — but on the power of governments (including school officials). As the *Mergens* Court stated, "there is a crucial difference between government speech endorsing religion, which the Establishment Clause forbids, and private speech endorsing religion, which the Free Speech and Free Exercise Clauses protect." [217]

APPENDIX II
KNOWING YOUR RIGHTS MEDIA GUIDE

Q What happens when I am contacted by the news media? How do I respond?

A In many communities, news reporters routinely cover local government activities, including school board meetings. For example, if you address a school board meeting, you may find that a reporter is in the audience. This presents an excellent opportunity to share your concerns with the school board and with the news media, which ultimately means the public. There are at least two sides to every story. You can bet the folks onthe other side of the issue will take advantage of an opportunity to tell their story to a reporter. You should too.

Q How do I handle such a request? What do I say to a reporter?

A The best way to handle a request from a news reporter is to be open and direct. Most reporters do not cover one topic. They bounce around, often covering a myriad of subjects in any given week. But even if they are covering a particular issue, they may still be unaware of your concerns on the issue and perhaps even ill-informed about the issue's intricacies. You can help educate the reporter, while at the same time taking advantage of an opportunity to express your side of the story. Be clear and concise. Make sure you know what you want to say and how you will say it. Get to the bottom line quickly. Focus on one or two key points.

Keep it simple. Do not get bogged down with too many details. Try to explain the essence of your position in a sentence or two. Reporters work under tight time and space limitations. They often must condense a complicated issue into a few sentences or paragraphs. Why not help them by being clear and concise? When you do, you increase your chances that the news coverage will be fair, balanced, and accurate.

Q How can I guarantee that my position will not be misstated? If I do not talk to a reporter, then I cannot be misquoted, right? Isn't that the best thing to do?

A There are no guarantees concerning the outcome of a news story. Believe it or not, most reporters are not conspiring to slant a story one way or the other. Most are professionals who strive to tell both sides of a story with balance and fairness. But, of course, you cannot be sure what information will be used and what information will be withheld. You certainly cannot be sure how it will be presented. But there is one thing you can know with certainty: If you do not offer your point of view and remain silent, you will have no input in the story. You will not be misquoted, but what could even be more damaging, you will not be quoted either. To compete equally in the marketplace of ideas, you must deal with the news media. You need to get your ideas and concerns into the marketplace, and one of the best ways to do that is through the media.

Q I do not want to be treated unfairly, though. How can I maximize the chances that my comments will be presented without bias? I just want to get a "fair shake."

A Again, the best approach is one of openness and clarity. Tell your story in a concise manner. There is nothing wrong with asking a reporter, "Do you understand what I am trying to say?" By asking that question, you give the reporter an opportunity to tell you how they perceive your position. Remember, communication is the key. You need to be direct, honest, and concise. Do not be afraid to repeat yourself. State your position. Re-state it. Re-state it again, if necessary. As I mentioned earlier, reporters often learn about a story as they are covering it. Help the education process along.

Be ready, willing, and able to provide a reporter with any additional information (written or otherwise) to help clarify and reinforce your position. Do not overload a reporter with a ream of documents, but a well-placed supporting document or two never hurts. In most instances, you will have just one opportunity to make your point. Take advantage of it.

Q All right, what happens if I participate and I am still misquoted? What do I do if the newspaper or TV news story is not accurate?

A The first thing you should do is stop and take a deep breath. If you feel the story was biased or unfair, you will likely be upset, angry, or worse. Calm down before you do anything. Before you take any action, ask yourself these questions: "Was the news story fair? Were both sides of the story presented and given equal treatment?" Re-read the story or play back the videotape before you answer. Notice I said both sides of the story. Sometimes we have a tendency to overreact and think a story is unfair because it includes criticism or opposition. Remember, a story is fair and balanced if it includes both sides of a story and treats both equally. A fair and balanced story should never be an advocacy piece for either side, including your own. If after considering all this, you still come to the conclusion the story was unfair, you should contact the reporter who did the story. Express your concerns in a calm fashion. No one likes to get a phone call from a screamer. Discuss the story and explain why you felt your position was misstated or treated unfairly. Use specifics. Remember, keep the lines of communication open. Do not threaten a reporter with a line like, "I will never talk to you again!" That may make you feel better, but it does not accomplish anything.

Your goal should be to develop trusting relationships with reporters and editors. That is right, I said trusting. The newspaper, radio, or television station is going to remain part of your community, and unless you decide to move away, you will no doubt deal with the media again. It will be to your advantage to get to know a reporter or a news editor. You do not have to become best buddies, but you need to talk with them, even when they are not doing a story that concerns you, developing a relationship with them, you will get to know them better, and more importantly, they will get to know you better. This builds trust. Trust helps keep the lines of communication open. And that is an important building block to fair and balanced news coverage.

By the way, if you think a reporter has done a good job with a story, pick up the phone and tell them. They like to hear that also.

Q If I have an interesting news story or would like some coverage about a specific event, what is the best way of going about contacting a reporter?

A The more comfortable you become dealing with the news media, the more likely you will want to initiate the contact. Remember, equal access to the marketplace of ideas means learning how to deal with the news media, and that should include being pro-active.

Reporters are always looking for news stories, and news stories center around ideas, issues, events, and people. You can alert reporters to potential news items and thereby become a valuable resource. So do not be afraid to initiate the contact. This is where developing a relationship with a reporter is very beneficial. If you know someone at the newspaper, radio or TV station, pick up the phone and give them a call. Let them know what is on your mind. Ask them who you should talk to about your potential story.

If you do not have a personal contact in the news department, try calling a news editor or an assignment editor. They are the decision-makers when it comes to covering a news story. Follow up the phone call with a letter or information that can be faxed to their attention. Remember, reporters have to work on tight schedules, so the faster they can get information, the better. Fax machines provide instant access. But do not abuse the opportunity. No news organization likes to be bombarded with a proliferation of lengthy news releases. Be selective of what you send, and keep it short.

One final note: Respect deadlines. If you call a reporter or an editor and he cannot talk to you, do not be offended. Chances are he is trying to beat a deadline. Ask him when it would be convenient for you to call back. As a general rule, avoid contacting news rooms in the late afternoon or early evening. That is when most reporters and editors are under the gun (particularly in the television industry). Generally, the best time to call reporters is early morning, after they have had their first cup of coffee.

ENDNOTES

1. *United States v. Kokinda*, 497 U.S. 720 (1990).
2. See *Lamb's Chapel v. Center Moriches Union Free School District*, 113 S.Ct. 2141 (1993).
3. *Hague v. Committee for Industrial Organization*, 307 U.S. 496, 515 (1939).
4. *Id.*, at 516.
5. *Id.*
6. *Forsythe County, Georgia v. Nationalist Movement*, 112 S.Ct. 2395 (1992), 505 U.S. 123.
7. See, *e.g., Lovell v. City of Griffin*, 303 U.S. 444 (1938).
8. *Kokinda*, 497 U.S. 720, 733-734 (1990).
9. *Id.*, at 734.
10. *Id.*
11. *Schneider v. State*, 308 U.S. 147 (1939).
12. *Id.*, at 162.
13. *Lamb's Chapel*, 113 S.Ct. 2141 (1993), 508 U.S. 384.
14. *Lynch v. Donnelly*, 465 U.S. 668 (1984); *Allegheny County v. American Civil Liberties Union, Greater Pittsburgh Chapter*, 492 U.S. 573 (1989).
15. *Lynch.*
16. *Allegheny County.*
17. *West Virginia v. Barnette*, 319 U.S. 624 (1943).
18. *Id.*, at 642.
19. *Capitol Square Review and Advisory Board v. Pinette*, ____ U.S. ____, 115 S.Ct. 2440, 132 L.Ed.2d 650 (1995).
20. *Id.*, at 2446.
21. *Id.*
22. *Id.*, at 2447.
23. *Id.*, at 2449.
24. *Id.*, at 2450

25. *The Club Southern Burlesque, Inc. v. The City of Rome, Georgia,* Case# 95-CV-2690-3.

26. *City of Renton v. Playtime Theatres, Inc.,* 475 U.S. 41,46 (1986).

27. *Id at* 51-52. *Niemotko v. Maryland* 340 U.S. 268 (1951); *Saia v. New York,* 334 U.S. 558.

28. *Westside Community Schools v. Mergens,* 496 U.S. 248 (1990).

29. *Tinker v. Des Moines Independent School District,* 393 U.S. 503 (1969).

30. *Good News/Good Sports Club v. School District of the City of Ladue,* 28 F.3d 1501 (8th Cir. 1994), cert. denied 115 S.Ct. 2640 (1995).

31. *Id.,* at 1509.

32. *Id.* (quoting *Westside Community Schools v. Mergens,* 496 U.S. 226, 248 (1990)).

33. *Id.,* at 1510.

34. *Rosenberger v. University of Virginia,* _____ U.S. _____, 115 S.Ct.2510, 132 L.Ed.2d. 700 (1995).

35. *Id.,* at 2514-15.

36. *Id.,* at 2515.

37. *Id.,* at 2519.

38. *Id.,* at 2521.

39. *Tinker.,* 509.

40. *Id.,* at 506.

41. *Id.,* at 513.

42. *Lee v. Weisman,* 112 S.Ct. 2649 (1992).

43. *Id.,* at 2655.

44. *Jones v. Clear Creek Independent School District,* 977 F.2d 963, 972 (5th Cir. 1992), cert. denied, 508 U.S. 967, 113 S.Ct. 2950, 124 L.Ed.2d 697 (1993) (*Jones II*).

45. *Id.,* at 963.

46. *Id.,* at 969 (citing *Mergens,* 496 U.S. 226, 250 (1990)).

47. *Harris v. Joint School District No. 241,* (Civ. No. 91-

0166-N-HLR), (D. Idaho May 20, 1993) (post-*Lee* decision upholding the right of students to initiate prayers at graduation).

48. F.3d 447 (9th Cir. 1994), *granted, vacated, and remanded* ___ U.S. ___, 115 S.Ct. 2604, 132 L.Ed.2d 849 (1995).

49. *Widmar v. Vincent*, 454 U.S. 263, 269 (1981) (citing *Heffron v. International Society for Krishna Consciousness, Inc.*, 452 U.S. 640 (1981)); *Westside Community Schools v. Mergens*, 496 U.S. 226 (1990); *Niemotko v. Maryland* 340 U.S. 268 (1951); *Saia v. New York*, 334 U.S. 558 (1948).

50. *Tinker*, 393 U.S. 503, 509 (1969).

51. *Widmar*, 454 U.S. 263 (1981).

52. *See Lamb's Chapel*, 113 S.Ct. 2141, 508 U.S. 384 (1993).

53. *Tinker*, 393 U.S. 503, 512-13 (1969).

54. *Id.*, at 506.

55. *Mergens*, 496 U.S. at 248. *Lamb's Chapel*, 113 S.Ct. 2141 (1993); *Grace Bible Fellowship, Inc. v. Maine School Admin. Dist. #5*, 941 F.2d 45 (1st Cir. 1991); *Gregoire v. Centennial School Dist.*, 907 F.2d 1366 (3d Cir.), *cert. denied*, 111 S.Ct. 253 (1990); *Concerned Women for America v. Lafayette County*, 883 F.2d 32 (5th Cir. 1989).

56. *Shumway v. Albany Co. School Dist. No. 1*, No. 93-CV-0153J (D. Wyo. filed June 9, 1993).

57. *Wallace v. Jaffree*, 472 U.S. 38 (1985).

58. *Id.*, at 62 (Powell, J. concurring) (citation and footnote omitted).

59. *Id.*, at 40 n.1.

60. *Id.*, at 59-61.

61. *Id.*, at 59-61.

62. *Tinker*, 393 U.S. at 513 (quoting *Burnside* at 749).

63. *Id.*

64. *Perry Educ. Assoc. v. Perry Local Educators' Assoc.*, 460 U.S. 37, 45 (1983).

65. *Florey v. Sioux Falls School Dist.*, 619 F.2d 1311, 1317 (8th Cir. 1980).

66. *Id.*, at 1314.

67. *School District of Abington Township v. Schempp*, 374 U.S. 203 (1963).

68. *Id.*, at 255.

69. *Stone v. Graham*, 449 U.S. 39, 42 (1980).

70. *Lamb's Chapel*, 113 S.Ct. 2141 (1993).

71. *Id.*, at 4552.

72. *See Lynch v. Donnelly*, 465 U.S. 668, 675, 680 (1984).

73. Teen-Aid, 723 East Jackson, Spokane, WA 99207, 509/482-2868;

74. United States Department of Education Guidelines, Richard W. Riley, Page 6.

75. *Id.*

76. *Id.*

77. *Id.*

78. *Id.*

79. *Id.* at 3.

80. *Id.*

81. *Id.*

82. *Id.*

83. *Id.*, at 4.

84. *Id.*

85. *Id.*

86. *Id.*

87. *Id.*

88. *Id.*, at 4 - 5.

89. *Id.*, at 4 - 5.

90. *Id.*

91. *Id.*

92. Id.

93. Id.

94. Id.

95. Id.

96. Id.

97. Title VII is codified at 42 U.S.C §§ 2000e et seq. It applies to virtually all employers with fifteen or more employees. For a more detailed explanation of Title VII, see Appendix I.

98. *Smith v. Pyro Mining*, 827 F.2d 1081, 1085 (6th Cir. 1987) cert. den., 485 U.S. 989 (1988); *Heller v. EBB Auto Co.*, 8 F3d 1433,

99. *Hansard v. Johns-Manville Products*, 5 EPD ¶ 8543 (E.D. Tex. 1973). Compare *Mississippi Employment Sec. Comm'n v. McGlothin*, 556 So. 2d 324 (Miss. 1990), cert. den., 111 S.Ct. 211 (1990) (employee's belief was sincerly held even though she was not an active member of her religious group and wore her head wrap only occasionally).

100. *Cooper v. General Dynamics*, 378 F. Supp. 1258 (N.D. Tex 1974), *rev'd on other grounds*, 533 F.2d 163 (5th Cir. 1976), cert. den., 433 U.S. 908 (1977).

101. *EEOC v. University of Detroit*, 701 F. Supp. 1326, 1331 (E.D. Mich. 1988), *rev'd. on other grounds*, 904 F.2d 331 (6th Cir. 1990).

102. *42 U.S.C. 2000c(j)*. The courts and the EEOC have interpreted this provision very liberally. Donald T. Kramer, Validity, Construction, and Application of Provisions of Title VII of the Civil Rights Act of 1964 (42 USCS §§ 2000c et seq.) and Implementing Regulations, Making Religious Discrimination in Employment Unlawful, 22 A.L.R. Fed. 580, 602 (1975)

103. *Guidlines On Discrimination Because of Religion*, 29 C.F.R. § 1605.1.

104. *Heller*, 8 F. 3d at 1438-39 (summarizing authorities); see also *Redmond v. GAF Corp.*, 574 F. 2d 897 (7th Cir. 1978); 22 A.L.R. Fed. at 601-03.

105. EEOC Dec. No. 71-2620 (1970); CCH EEOC Dec ¶ 6823; *EEOC* Dec.¶ 6180; EEOC Dec. No. 72-1301 (1972); *CCH EEOC* Dec. ¶ 6338; *Young v. Southwestern Sav. & Loan Assoc.*, 509 F.2d 140 (5th Cir. 1975)

106. *EEOC* Dec. No. 79-06 (1978), *CCH EEOC* Dec. 6737;, 368 F. Supp. 1025 (E.D. Va. 1973), aff'd., 508 F.2d 504 (4th Cir. 1974); *Brown v. Pena*, 441 F. Supp. 1382 (S.D. Fla. 1977), aff'd, 589 F.2d 1113 (5th Cir. 1982).

107. *Heller*, 8 F.3d at 1439.

108. *Brown v. Polk County*, 61 F.3d 650, 654-55(8th Cir. 1995), cert. den., 116 S. Ct. 1042 (1996).

109. See *Chalmers v. Tulon Co.*, 101 F.3d 1012 (4th Cir. 1996).

110. *Chrysler Corp. v. Mann*, 561 F.2d 1282, 1285-86 (8th Cir. 1977), cert. den., 434 U.S. 1039 (1978).

111. Gregory S. Sarno, Harassment or Termination of Employee Due to Religious Beliefs or Practices, 35 P.O.F.2d 209, 222 (1983) (hereinafter "Harassment"); *EEOC v. Townley Eng'g and Mfg.*, 859 F.2d 610, 614 n.5 (4th Cir. 1988), cert den., 489 U.S. 1077 (1989).

112. *Trans World Airlines v. Hardison*, 432 U.S. 63, 73-74 (1977); *EEOC v. READS, Inc.*, 759 F. Supp. 1150, 1155 (E.D. Pa. 1991); 29 C.F.R. § 1605.2(c).

113. *Riley v. Bendix Corp.*, 464 F.2d 1113, 1115 (5th Cir. 1972); *Reid v. Memphis Publishing Co.*, 468 F.2d 346, 350-51 (6th Cir. 1972) (the fact that a particular policy is applied uniformly to all employees does not lessen the discriminatory effect upon a particular employee's religious beliefs).

114. *Brown*, 61 F.3d at 652.

115. *Id.* at 657 (quoting *Burns v. Southern Pacific Transit Co.*, 589 F.2d 403, 407 (9th Cir. 1978), cert. den., 439 U.S. 1072 (1979)). See also *EEOC* Dec. ¶ 6674 (1976), where an Orthodox Muslim was unlawfully fired for being "overzealous in his practices of his beliefs in his conversa-

tion with officers and inmates." The employer fired him because he "cannot be persuaded to tone down his religious practices on the job and continually gets wrapped up in conversations with the inmates." Because there was no evidence that the employee's conduct had made him unable to perform his duties or hampered the efficient operation of the workplace, the employee prevailed in his claim.

116. *CCH EEOC* Dec. ¶ 6338.

117. In re: *Broadbelt*, 146 N.J. 501, 683 A.2d 543 (1996), cert. den., 117 S. Ct. 1251 (1997); See also *Hollon v. Pierce*, 64 Cal. Rptr. 808 (Cal. Ct. App. 1967) (California human rights law was not violated by dismissal of school transportation supervisor who had, wholly apart from his employment, produced and distributed a religious tract that led school district to question supervisor's mental stability).

118. *Lake v. B.F. Goodrich Co.*, 837 F.2d 449 (11th Cir. 1988), cert. den., 488 U.S. 826 (1988).

119. *Id.* at 451. See also *E.E.O.C. v. Hacienda Hotel*, 881 F.2d 1504 (9th Cir. 1989) (employer violated Title VII when it made no effort to accommodate two employees' requests to be off on their Sabbaths).

120. *Brown v. General Motors*, 601 F.2d 956, 959 (8th Cir. 1979). See also *Protos v. Volkswagen of America*, 797 F.2d 129 (3rd Cir. 1986) cert. den., 479 U.S. 972.

121. *E.E.O.C. v. Universal Mfg.*, 914 F.2d 71 (5th Cir. 1990).

122. *Pyro Mining*, 827 F.2d 1081- 1086.

123. *Haring v. Blumenthal*, 471 F. Supp. 1172 (D.D.C. 1979), cert. den., 452 U.S. 939 (1981) reh'g den. 453 U.S. 927 (1981).

124. *Kentucky Comm'n on Human Rights v. Lesco Mfg. & Design Co.*, 736 S.W.2d 361 (Ky. Ct. App. 1987).

125. See *McDaniel v. Essex International, Inc.*, 571

F.2d 338 (6th Cir. 1978), on remand, 509 F. Supp. 1055 (W.D. Mich. 1981), aff'd, 696 F.2d 34 (6th Cir. 1982); *Tooley v. Martin-Marietta Corp.*, 648 F.2d 1239 (9th Cir. 1981), cert. den., 454 U.S. 1098 (1981).

126. University of Detroit, 701 F. Supp. at 1341, rev'd. on other grounds, 904 F.2d 331 (6th Cir. 1990).

127. *EEOC* Dec. ¶ 6180 (1970). See also *EEOC* Dec. ¶ 6283 (1971) (where an employer could not fire employee for wearing traditional Islam garb because there was no evidence that requiring employees to wear traditional office attire was necessary to the safe and efficient operation of the business).

128. *Wilson v. U.S. West Communications*, 58 F.3d 1337 (8th Cir. 1995). However, the court in this case found that the employee's religious belief that she must wear a Pro-Life button depicting a fetus was reasonably accommodated when the employer offered to let the employee wear the button as long as it was covered, or let the employee wear a button with a similar message, but without the picture of the fetus.

129. *EEOC* Dec. ¶6817 (1982). See also *Bhatia v. Chevron USA, Inc.*, 734 F.2d 1382 (9th Cir. 1984).

130. See, e.g., *Minnesota Dept. of Highways v. Minnesota Dept. of Human Rights*, 11 EPD ¶ 10863 (1976).

131. *Smith v. Universal Services*, 360 F. Supp. 441 (E.D. La. 1972) (Where the court dismissed the complaint of a Pentecostal Church member who claimed he was fired because while he worked he sang religious hymns, preached, and prophesied of disasters and the death of co-workers on the job. The court found that his inability to get along with other employees and poor work were the reasons plaintiff was fired, and not his religious speech). See also *Gillard v. Sears Roebuck & Co.*, 32 FEP 1274 (E.D. Pa. 1983).

132. *EEOC* Decision No. 91-1 (1991).

133. See, e.g., Redmond, 574 F.2d at 901-2; *Opuku-Boateng v. State of California*, 95 F.3d 1461, 1473-74 (9th Cir. 1996), cert.den., 520 U.S. 1228 (1997). *Shaffeld v. Northrop Worldwide Aircraft Serv. Inc.*, 373 F. Supp. 937, 944 (M.D. Ala. 1974).

134. *Pyro Mining*, 827 F.2d at 1086; Haring, 471 F. Supp. at 1182 ("'undue hardship' must mean present undue hardship, as distinguished from anticipated or multiplied hardship" (emphasis in original)).

135. *Anderson v. General Dynamics Convair Aerospace Div.*, 589 F.2d 397, 402 (9th Cir. 1978) cert. den. 442 U.S. 921 (1979); Burns, 589 F.2d 403 at 406; *Cummins v. Parker Seal Co.*, 516 F.2d 544, 548 (6th Cir. 1975), aff'd, 429 U.S. 65 (1976), vacated and remanded for reh'g, 403 U.S. 903 (1977).

136. *Pyro Mining*, 827 F.2d at 1085-86 (quoting *Draper v. United States Pipe & Foundry Co.*, 527 F.2d 515, 520 (6th Cir. 1975)). However, "the mere existence of a seniority system does not relieve an employer of the duty to attempt reasonable accommodation of its employees' religious practices...." *Balint v. Carson City, Nevada,* 180 F.3d 1047, 1049 (9th Cir. 1999).

137. Trans World Airlines, 432 U.S. at 84; *Turpen v. Missouri-Kansas-Texas R. Co.*, 736 F.2d at 1027.

138. *Dixon v. Omaha Public Power District*, 385 F. Supp. 1382 (D. Neb. 1974). See also *United States v. City of Albuquerque*, 423 F. Supp. 591 (D.N.M. 1975), aff'd, 545 F.2d 110 (10th Cir. 1976), cert. den., 433 U.S. 909 (1977) (where accommodating fireman's Sabbath would have required other firefighters to work 38 hour shifts).

139. *Westside Community Schools v. Mergens*, 496 U.S. 226, 250 (1990).

140. *Perry v. Sindermann*, 408 U.S. 593 (1972); *Rutan v. Republican Party of Illinois*, 497 U.S. 62 (1990).

141. *Connick v. Myers*, 461 U.S. 138, 147 (1983).

142. *Pickering v. Board of Education*, 391 U.S. 563, 568 (1968).

143. 97 F.3d 1204 (9th Cir. 1996).

144. *Brown*, 61 F.3d at 659.

145. *Id.*

146. *Tucker*, 97 F.3d at 1215.

147. *Id.*

148. *Brown*, 61 F.3d at 659.

149. *McDaniel v. Paty*, 435 U.S. 618, 641 (1978) (Brennan, J., concurring).

150. *Brown*, 61 F.3d at 659. (quoting Whitney v. California, 274 U.S. 376 (1927)(Brandeis, J. concurring)).

151. Guidelines on Religious Exercise and Religious Expression in the Federal Workplace, August 22, 1997, available in, WESTLAW, 1997 WL 13652877.

152. *Brown v. Polk County*, 61 F.3d 650 (8th Cir. 1995), cert. den., 116 S. Ct. 1042 (1996).

153. *E.E.O.C. v. Townley Engineering & Mfg. Co.*, 859 F.2d 610, 621 (9th Cir. 1988).

154. *Meltebeke v. Bureau of Labor & Indus.*, 903 P.2d 351, 362-63 (Or. 1995) (evangelical Christian employer did not violate state law prohibiting employers from "making religious advances" by witnessing to his employee and inviting him to church).

155. *Chalmers,* 101 F.3d at 1021.

156. *Taylor v. National Group of Co's.*, 729 F. Supp. 575 (N.D. Ohio 1989) (employer's gift of a book endorsing secular humanism to new employees on their first day of work did not rise to the level of religious discrimination against a Christian employee).

157. *Brown Transport Corp. v. Human Relations Com'n.*, 578 A.2d 555 (Pa. Commw. Ct. 1990).

158. *Young v. Southwestern Sav. & Loan Assoc.*, 509 F.2d 140 (5th Cir. 1975).

159. *Brown v. Polk County*, 61 F.3d 650 (8th Cir.

1995), cert. den., 116 S. Ct. 1042 (1996).
160. *Kolodziej v. Smith*, 588 N.E.2d 634 (Mass. 1992).
161. *Armbruster v. Quinn*, 711 F.2d 1332, 1342 (6th Cir. 1983).
162. *Brown v. GSA*, 425 U.S. 820, 835 (1976); *Church of Scientology v. Director, FBI*, 459 F. Supp. 748, 759 (D.C. DC 1978).
163. 42 U.S.C. § 2000e-5(e)(1).
164. Title VII time limits "are not jurisdictional." *Oshiver v. Levin, Fishbein, Sedran & Berman*, 38 F.3d 1380, *City of Albuquerque*, 423 F. Supp. 591 (D.N.M. 1975), aff'd, 545 F.2d 110 (10th Cir. 1976), cert. den., 433 U.S. 909 (1977) (where accommodating fireman's Sabbath would have required other firefighters to work 38 hour shifts). 1387 (3d Cir. 1994). The limits are analogous to statutes of limitation and are subject to equitable modification. Id.; see also *Rice v. New England College*, 676 F.2d 9, 10 (1st Cir. 1982). Equitable modifications were permitted where "a claimant has received inadequate notice; or where a motion for appointment of counsel is pending...; or where the court has led the plaintiff to believe that she had done everything required of her [or] affirmative misconduct on the part of a defendant...." *Baldwin County Welcome Center v. Brown*, 466 U.S. 147, 151 (1984) (citations omitted). In contrast, modification was not permitted where a pro se claimant argued the right-to-sue letter was ambiguous, *Soto v. U.S. Postal Serv.*, 905 F.2d 537 (1st Cir. 1990) cert. den., 498 U.S. 1027 (1991); the claimant misunderstood the right-to-sue letter and named the wrong defendant, *Rys v. U.S. Postal Serv.*, 886 F.2d 443 (1st Cir. 1989); or where the claimant filed claims well after the 180 day period despite sufficient knowledge of procedures and fora for administrative relief. *Hamilton v. West*, 30 F.3d 992, 993-94 (8th Cir. 1994).

165. *Id.*
166. 42 U.S.C. § 2000e-(5)(d).
167. See *Breen v. Norwest Bank Minnesota, N.A.*, 865 F. Supp. 574, 578 (D.Minn. 1994) (complaint untimely when deferral agency did not cross-file complaint and plaintiff's counsel failed to monitor filings).
168. 42 U.S.C. § 2000e-5(f)(1).
169. *Id.*
170. *Id.*
171. *Id.*
172. 29 C.F.R. § 1614.105(a)(1)(1996).
173. §1614.105(a)(2)(d).
This period is extended to 90 days if the agency has a "dispute resolution procedure" in place, §1614.105(a)(2)(f), or for up to 60 days if the aggrieved person so requests in writing. § 1614.105(a)(2)(e).
174. *Id.*
175. § 1614.108(f).
176. § 1614.408(b).
177. § 1614.408(a).person so requests in writing. § 1614.105(a)(2)(e).
178. § 1614.402(a).
179. § 1614.406.
180. § 1614.408(d).
181. *Tinker v. Des Moines Independent School District*, 393 U.S. 503, 506 (1969).
182. *Westside Community Schools v. Mergens*, 867 F.2d 1076 (1989),
183. *Tinker* at 509 (quoting *Burnside v. Byars*, 363 F.2d 744, 749 (5th Cir. 1966)).
184. *Tinker*, at 506.
185. *Id.*, at 512-13.
186. *Tinker*, at 511 (quoting *Burnside*, at 749).
187. *Id.*, at 509.
188. *Widmar v. Vincent*, 454 U.S. 263, 269 (1981)

(citing *Heffron v. International Society for Krishna Consciousness, Inc.*, 452 U.S. 640 (1981)); *Westside Community Schools v. Mergens*, 496 U.S. 226 (1990); *Niemotko v. Maryland*, 340 U.S. 268 (1951); and *Saia v. New York*, 334 U.S. 558 (1948).

189. *Thomas v. Collins*, 323 U.S. 516, 537 (1945) (emphasis added)

190. *Widmar*, 454 U.S. 263 (1981)

191. *Garnett v. Renton School Dist. No. 403*, 987 F.2d 641 (9th Cir. 1993)

192. *Westside Community Schools v. Mergens*, 496 U.S. 226 (1990)

193. *Id.*, at 239-40.

194. *Id.* (quoting *McDaniel v. Paty*, 435 U.S. 618, 641 (1978) (Brennan, J., concurring in judgment)).

195. *Id.*, at 247.

196. *Lovell v. City of Griffin*, 303 U.S. 444 (1938); *Widmar*, 454 U.S. 263, 269 (1981).

197. *Rivera v. East Otero School District R-1*, 721 F. Supp. 1189, 1194 (D.Colo. 1989) (citation omitted).

198. *Lovell*, 303 U.S. 444; *Heffron v. International Society for Krishna Consciousness*, 452 U.S. 640 (1981).

199. *Lovell*, 303 U.S. at 452 (emphasis added) (citations omitted).

200. *Lovell*, 303 U.S at 448.

201. *Murdock*, 319 U.S. at 108-09 (1943) (footnotes omitted).

202. *United States v. Kokinda*, 497 U.S. 720, 734 (1990) (plurality).

203. *Id.*

204. *Tinker*, 393 U.S. 508.

205. *Id.*, at 514.

206. *See Rivera v. East Otero School District R-1*, 721 F. Supp. 1189 (D. Colo. 1989); *Thompson v. Waynesboro Area School District*, 673 F. Supp. 1379 (N.D. Pa. 1987);

Nelson v. Moline School District No. 40, 725 F. Supp. 965 (C.D. Ill. 1989); *Hemry v. School Board of Colorado Springs School District 11*, 760 F. Supp. 856 (D. Colo. 1991).

207. *Hemry v.School Board of Colorado Springs*, No.90-S-2188, Stipulation for Dismissal (D. Colo. Sept. 1991) (unpublished). *Accord Harden v. School Board of Pinellas County*, No. 901544-CIV-T-15A, Consent Decree and Order (M.D. Fla. 1991) (students permitted to distribute religious newspaper on campus).

208. *Tinker*, 393 U.S. at 511.

209. *Rivera*, 721 F. Supp. at 1193.

210. *Tinker*, 393 U.S. at 512-13.

211. *Rivera*, at 1197.

212. *See Tinker*, 393 U.S. at 512. Also, *Hemry* does not contravene this proposition. The *Hemry* court clearly stated that the facts of the case before it were distinguishable from the facts in *Rivera*. *Hemry* at 859. Because the school in *Hemry* did not ban literature, but only enforced reasonable time, place, and manner restrictions, the court did apply a forum analysis. Nonetheless, *Tinker* and *Rivera* still stand for the proposition that literature distribution cannot be banned in public schools, regardless of what type of forum they constitute. As noted above, the final disposition of *Hemry* resulted in a Stipulation for Dismissal which allowed unregulated personal distribution of literature and mass distribution subject only to reasonable time, place, and manner restrictions. Stipulation for Dismissal (D. Colo. Nov. 12, 1991) (unpublished).

213. *West Virginia v. Barnette*, 319 U.S. 624, 637 (1943).

214. *Id.*, at 637.

215. *Shelton v. Tucker*, 364 U.S. 479, 487 (1967).

216. *Mergens*, at 249-50 (citation omitted) (emphasis added).

217. *Mergens*, 496 U.S. at 250 (emphasis in original).